TWELVE STEPS FOR WHITE AMERICA

WORKBOOK

TWELVE STEPS FOR WHITE AMERICA

WILLIAM WATSON

Printed in the United States of America.

Call

The only thing white people have that black people need, or should want, is power—and no one holds power forever. White people cannot, in the generality, be taken as models of how to live. Rather, the white man is himself in sore need of new standards, which will release him from his confusion and place him once again in fruitful communion with the depths of his own being.

James Baldwin
The Fire Next Time

Response

May Twelve Steps for White America *provide standards that place White Americans once again in fruitful communion with the depths of our being.*

William Watson

STATEMENT ON ALCOHOLICS ANONYMOUS AND THE SPIRITUAL FOUNDATION OF ANONYMITY

Application of the Underlying Problem-Solving Principles

The principles that form the foundation of the 12 steps presented in Alcoholics Anonymous (AA), are basic problem-solving principles universal to the human condition. Humanity survives because we learn and practice and continuously transfer problem-solving principles that enable us to adapt and survive. Universal problem-solving principles, fundamental to the human condition, pre-date AA. They are catalogued and represented by AA as a revolution in the treatment of alcoholism.

The AA representation of these underlying problem-solving principles in the form of 12 steps revolutionized the treatment of alcoholism in the 20th century. When referred to throughout this work, the AA 12 steps are sourced appropriately. While AA presents those universal problem-solving principles as a treatment plan for the *dysfunction/disorder of alcoholism,* I present those universal problem-solving principles as a treatment plan for the *national dysfunction/disorder of rigged advantage,* which threatens our democracy.

Anonymity

I share only what is mine to share—my lived experience of practicing recovery principles in all my affairs. I do not speak for Alcoholics Anonymous. I do not represent AA in any way. I am not identifying as a "member" of AA. I do not share anything in this book as if I am a "member" of AA. I should not be considered as an example of what an AA member was, is, or could be. First copyrighted in 1952 by A.A. Grapevine, Inc. and Alcoholics Anonymous Publishing (now known as Alcoholics Anonymous World Services), the *Twelfth Tradition*[1] (different from the *Twelfth Step*) is a hallowed principle that mitigated a stigma in the early and mid-20th century that may be nearly unimaginable to 21st-century sensibilities. Still, today, it is remains as important as it was then.

> *Anonymity is the spiritual foundation of all our traditions, ever reminding us to place principles before personalities.*[2]

1 A.A. World Services, Inc. (1989). *The twelve steps and twelve traditions: A co-founder of Alcoholics Anonymous tells how members recover and how the society functions.* Author. (Originally published in 1952). (p. 184)
2 A.A. World Services, Inc. (1989). *The twelve steps and twelve traditions: A co-founder of Alcoholics Anonymous tells how members recover and how the society functions.* (Originally published in 1952). (p. 184)

DETAILED CONTENTS

DEDICATION IN MEMORY

In Memory of Helga Burnham Watson and Hubert Watson

Twelve Steps for White America is dedicated to
The Honorable Constance Slaughter-Harvey

Twelve Steps for White America is dedicated to a living legend. The Honorable Constance Slaughter-Harvey is an iconic Mississippi civil rights attorney lauded alongside Fannie Lou Hamer and Leontyne Price as one of 10 notable Mississippi women of the 20th century.[1] Constance Slaughter-Harvey ascended to unimaginable heights of political achievement in an era when integrating the University of Mississippi (known as "Ole Miss," a term for the "mistress" of a slavery plantation)[2] precipitated the intervention of the U.S. Supreme Court, the Kennedy administration, and a federalized National Guard for James Meredith to enroll amid rioting.

Mississippi Governor Ross Barnett taunted Attorney General Robert Kennedy and President Kennedy, pontificating that this was "our greatest crisis since the war between the states."[3] The governor's crisis was a Black man enrolling at Ole Miss—not the backlash riot. James Meredith's 1962 televised trail-blazing required a military-style occupation of the Ole Miss college town, Oxford, Mississippi. Rowan Oak, William Faulkner's home in Oxford, remains a literary tourist attraction.[4] Faulkner's nephew, a captain in the federalized Mississippi National Guard, protected Meredith from the mob of violent White insurrectionists, defending their way of life from democracy's march forward.[5]

Constance Slaughter followed this "greatest crisis since the war between the states"[6] to enroll at the University of Mississippi School of Law. An unabashed pantheon of White patriarchal supremacy, the

---

1 Beveridge, L. (2020, August 26). Civil rights activist Fannie Lou Hamer and opera singer Leontyne Price among inspiring women on Mississippi list. *USA Today*. https://www.usatoday.com/in-depth/life/women-of-the-century/2020/08/13/mississippi-woman-history-poet-author-activists-19th-amendment/5003960002/

2 Parry, M. (2019, November 8). The trouble with Ole Miss. *The Chronicle of Higher Education*. https://www.chronicle.com/article/the-trouble-with-ole-miss/

3 U.S. Department of Justice. (2021). *The U.S. Marshals and the integration of the University of Mississippi*. U.S. Marshal Service. https://www.usmarshals.gov/history/miss/02.htm

4 www.rowanoak.com

5 U.S. Department of Justice. (2021). *The U.S. Marshals and the integration of the University of Mississippi*. U.S. Marshal Service. https://www.usmarshals.gov/history/miss/02.htm

6 Doyle's 2001 book (Doubleday) describing these events is titled *An American Insurrection, the Battle of Oxford Mississippi, 1962*. Interestingly, this is how the January 6, 2021, insurrection is characterized. A state CEO manipulates racialized undercurrents to incite riot against "x" (backlash) so that the status quo (sustained by White supremacy) benefits elite White Americans in power. Certifying Biden's win by over 7 million votes the day after a historical slave state elects two senators—one Jewish, one African American—is a templated replay of the "crisis" of James Meredith enrolling at Ole Miss. This repeat is not a "what's happening to our country" moment. It is a predictable playbook tactic that persists because the United States has never repented and atoned for slavery. We keep doing it. Slavery legacies are alive in the present. White Americans are responsible for dismantling the rigged advantage the flows to them to this day from the legacies of slavery. The United States remains at risk on this fault line, compromised until a repair is complete. *Twelve Steps for White America* outlines the steps needed for the repair.

Ole Miss law school reigned as a reliable status quo progenitor of racialized hatred in Mississippi.[7] In that world, Constance Slaughter triumphed as the first African American woman to earn a law degree from the University of Mississippi School of Law, where the Confederate rebel and Confederate flag were mascot and banner. Her courageous and inspiring career produced a domino effect of firsts across Mississippi history becoming the first African American woman judge and then the first African American assistant secretary of state/general counsel, serving for 12 years.

Early on, I only knew "Connie" as the daughter of that nice lady owner of the Six Cees Superette, Mrs. Olivia Kelly Slaughter, who quoted Shakespeare. Connie's father, Mr. W. L. Slaughter, was an esteemed educational administrator and Forest, Mississippi, alderman, who earned a master's degree from the University of California, Los Angeles (UCLA) after losing his left hand in WWII.[8] When you could buy gas at the Six Cees Superette for 32 cents per gallon,[9] my country parents and the impressive and accomplished Slaughters worked for local change when Connie (one of the six Slaughter daughters of the Superette's six "Cees")[10] was becoming a historical juggernaut for justice. "Local change" is my euphemism for my parents' life-risking voter registration drives, community organizing with the Scott County Improvement Association, and working with Mississippi Action for Progress to launch Head Start in Lauderdale, Scott, and Neshoba Counties. Freedom Summer's Chaney, Goodman, and Schwerner had recently been murdered there by the KKK colluding with law enforcement,[11] events portrayed in the film *Mississippi Burning*.[12]

Years later in Oakland, California, I met Black Panther Party cofounder, Bobby Seale, who delivered the commencement address where I was a college vice president. He spoke as an elder statesman recalling the Black Panther Party's Free Breakfast Program for school children and voter registration drives. Afterward, in our brief encounter, I referenced his address saying that in the '60s, Mother and Daddy had worked in voter registration drives in Mississippi. This legendary Black Panther raised his knowing eyebrows and said, "They were some brave people."

His empathic words broke open my soul. Cloaked in academic doctoral regalia, I might as well have been 10 years old, barefooted on a dirt road, twitchy after the Klan threatened to kill us. Triggered raw, faded fear flooded me. I cried hot tears to heaven on the way home, praying, "I hope y'all heard that—the cofounder of the Black Panther Party said y'all were brave." Short but so sweet; it was an extraordinary source of validation uttered for my parents. They worked exposed and threatened,

---

7 Stanford University Law School. (2021). *ABA women trailblazer's project*. Robert Crown Law Library. https://abawtp.law.stanford.edu/exhibits/show/constance-i-slaughter-harvey/biography?_ga=2.110698829.914675179.1597941222-1936040103.1597615574

8 Stanford University Law School. (2021). *ABA women trailblazer's project*. Robert Crown Law Library. https://abawtp.law.stanford.edu/exhibits/show/constance-i-slaughter-harvey/biography?_ga=2.110698829.914675179.1597941222-1936040103.1597615574

9 U.S. Office of Energy Efficiency & Renewable Energy. (2016). *Fact #915: March 7, 2016 average historical annual gasoline pump price, 1929–2015*. https://www.energy.gov/eere/vehicles/fact-915-march-7-2016-average-historical-annual-gasoline-pump-price-1929-2015

10 Scott County Times Online. (2018). Slaughter Legacy honored: Forest Alderman W. L. and Mrs. Olivia Kelley Slaughter honored (posthumously) by Jackson Tougaloo Alumni Club. *Scott County Times*. https://www.sctonline.net/front-page-slideshow-features/slaughter-legacy-honored#st-hash.74ptwXBg.dpbs

11 Ownby, T. (2017). *Mississippi Action for Progress (MAP)*. Center for Study of Southern Culture, Mississippi Encyclopedia. http://mississippiencyclopedia.org/entries/mississippi-action-for-progress/

12 FBI History. (1964). *Mississippi burning*. https://www.fbi.gov/history/famous-cases/mississippi-burning

largely uncredited for their sacrifice, shrouded in a tamping Whiteness that settles even the Civil War as simply "the late unpleasantness."[13]

As I grew older, I appreciated Constance Slaughter beyond family friend Connie, whom my parents adored. I came to know her better after I graduated from high school, and, as one does, dropped out of university to enter a psychiatric hospital diagnosed with depression (undiagnosed alcoholism, actually). Surely out of love and sympathy for my parents' grasping for what to do, Connie hired me to do some office work, where, early in her career, she had founded East Mississippi Legal Services as executive director. Through my haze of psychiatric meds, I can hardly remember any of it. What I do know is that her dignity and investment in my future mitigated my nightmare of alcoholism and depression, lighting a way forward beyond my immediate demoralization at a teetering time of life. Grateful, I became a fan of the history-making Constance Slaughter. Mother and I attended her wedding celebration at LeFleur's Restaurant in Jackson, Mississippi. Thereafter, she became known to history as Constance Slaughter-Harvey.

I learned more about my parents' affections for Connie and appreciated the mutuality of their relationship when she eulogized my father in 2007 and later visited my mother regularly in nursing care until she passed in 2013. It was a great honor for someone of Constance Slaughter-Harvey's status to eulogize my father. The son of outhouse-poor racist sharecroppers, he ran away from his life before completing high school. Proffered by an African American civil rights legend in a southern White country church pulpit, the transcendent symbolism of just her presence credited sacrifice to a man who once told me, "You can go to church with them racist som-bitches if you want to—I'd rather go to hell." Laughter erupts easily at a southern funeral as it did when Connie referenced his well-known obsession with "them goddam Republicans." In retrospect, it was funnier as obsession then, than as prophecy now.

A few years later at Mother's funeral, Connie revealed to me that Mother was already a member of the NAACP "when Medgar was killed." Those were hallowed words of respect from Connie, who, inspired by Medgar Evers, marched in his tragic funeral procession only 10 days after she met him.[14] The day Mother died, the Mississippi House of Representatives adjourned in her honor. I knew who made that happen. The Democratic Party's Resolution hailed Mother as "Lady Warrior."[15] This was the fiercely moral social justice mother I knew—not the sweet old quirky lady from her "White"-washed eulogy.

After Mother's funeral, waiting at Reagan International to board a flight home to San Francisco, I opened my wallet to give my credit card to a café's chatty, sweet server. Surprised by the unexpected, she said, "I hope you don't mind me asking, but I noticed the NAACP membership card in your wallet and I'm just curious." I explained, "Every time I open my wallet, it reminds me of who I am and where

13 McDavid, I. R., Jr., & McDavid, V. G. (1969). The late unpleasantness: Folk names for the Civil War. *The Southern Speech Journal, 34*(3), 194–204, https://doi.org/10.1080/10417946909372004
14 Sadoff, J. H., Sadoff, R. L., & Needleman, L. (2011). *Pieces from the past: Voices of heroic women in civil rights*. Tasora Books.
15 Clark, H., & Knowles, C. (2013). *Resolution in memory of Helga Burnham Watson*. Scott County Democratic Executive Committee.

I'm from. Mother was a Yellow-Dog Democrat who would expect me to be a card-carrying member. She was already a member of the NAACP 'when Medgar was killed.'"

Even now, as an "expat" of Mississippi for many years, the stifling inching of Mississippi time, the Slaughters, the Watsons, the NAACP "making democracy work since 1909," the voter registration drives, MAP Head Start, James Meredith-Ole Miss, twitchy bare feet on dirt roads, my precarious coming of age, and the Honorable Constance Slaughter-Harvey all burnish in sagas of memory—a legacy of the price already paid and the debt still due. As Faulkner wrote in *Requiem for a Nun,*

"The past is never dead. It's not even past."

ACKNOWLEDGMENTS

August 14, 1987, Winfried L. took me to Loyola University in the New Orleans Garden District for an AA Big Book study with notable AA teachers, Joe M. and Charlie P. I lost the Big Book I started out with a few months earlier. While at Loyola for the Big Book Study, I bought my new Big Book, the third edition, which has been with me ever since. It is raggedy and splotchy. The cover is long gone. The yellowed pages are filled with spectacular notes that captured the insights of the Joe and Charlie duo known throughout the recovery world for their illuminating insights into AA history and practical application of the steps.

Winfried (Vin-freed) would put his German accent face within about 6 inches of my face with his pointed finger in between to "tell me a thing or two" about how I was not going to stay sober doing x, y, and z. Of course, I couldn't stand him—and, of course, that was irrelevant. The entire recovery experience has been something I can't stand! But, to get sober, you must "act yourself into the right way of thinking," not the other way around. "Tolerating" Winfried left me with a Joe and Charlie–filled Big Book I still study 35 years later. It is the treasure trove I used to write this book. We lost touch years ago, but, while writing this book, I learned that Winfried had passed away. Confounded when learning the news of his passing, my heart held two things to be true at the same time: I couldn't stand him, and I am so grateful to him for the rigor he contributed to my sobriety.

Thank you to Lauren Sneed at San Francisco State University for her years of professional support, and for introducing me to Rebecca Toporek at San Francisco State University. Dr. Toporek's discussions with me about this work in the earliest stages proved very valuable.

Thank you to the iconic Honorable Constance Slaughter-Harvey, Hubert and Helga's beloved Connie.

Thank you to Dr. Christine Sleeter for her luminous integrity, a how-to-live masterclass.

Thank you to Yogacharya Ellen Grace O'Brian, whose *Jewel of Abundance* was the text for my inward journey, a pandemic-stillness spirit quest, which immediately preceded the writing of this book.

Thank you to Nicole Anderson, Heather Smith Bettini, Dr. Joi Lin Blake, Adolfo Leiva, and Dr. Anne Palmer. Thank you to my extraordinary colleagues in the Aspen Presidential Fellowship for being great human beings whose "fellowship" facilitated profound professional validation.

Thank you to James Ball for 21 years and to Ella Rose for joy every day.

Thank you to a great team at Cognella Press for this opportunity.

12SWA TOOLKIT

ESSENTIAL TOOLS FOR LEARNING AND PRACTICING 12SWA

WHO SHOULD READ THE BOOK *TWELVE STEPS FOR WHITE AMERICA*?

Before you conclude this is a funny question in the tradition of "Who is Buried in Grant's Tomb,"
let's just say,
It's complicated!
Obviously, the category White is in the title of the book, but let's talk about that briefly now.
"The book is intended for White Americans" is *an* answer, but *the* answer is more complex.

The *Twelve Steps for White America* are about dismantling rigged advantage, which requires more than just a group of individual White Americans. White American individuals are necessary but insufficient to dismantle rigged advantage. This work involves an entire culture of organizations, traditions, laws, systems, beliefs, habits, and more.

However, the book emphasizes "White America" for a reason. The book assumes that since the category we refer to as White America has benefitted from rigged advantage, White Americans should work categorically to dismantle rigged advantage. The burden for dismantling rigged advantage should not be placed on the very backs of those whom the system is rigged against.

INDIVIDUAL VS GROUP

What is true for "my group" may or may not be true for "me."

Re: My Group

White American households may be 8 times wealthier than Black American households.

Re: Me

My White household may be struggling, and the Black CEO where I work is a multi-millionaire.

1. **"Who is White?" and "How does White work?"**

   WHO: Throughout American history, "who is White" has evolved from "no Brit or European was referred to as White in the early history of Virginia" to today, where the category White includes more people than the category included, even at the end of the 19th century.

   HOW: Since median household wealth in the United States is 8 times higher for White households than Black households, "how White works" is a dysfunction that the future of a United States of America cannot afford to remain competitive or secure in the world.

2. **Since most White Americans share the same interests with "other" Americans regarding what they need to thrive,**

   Why do "many Whites" align with the interests of a few elite Whites against "many Whites" self-interest?
   Who does this manufactured alignment serve?
   Who does not want me to answer these questions?

3. **Since "who" may feel so complicated, let's oversimplify this for now, to say what is still a mouthful:**

   My personal struggle may not *feel* rigged. Still, the *category* of all White America is rigged for an elite portion of White America who rely on my White affinity to sustain their elite advantage.

IN-A-NUTSHELL GRAPHIC FOR CLARITY AND PERSPECTIVE

If at any point you get lost while working these steps, return to this graphic to visualize the big picture. Keeping your perspective helps with focus and understanding.

TWELVE STEPS FOR WHITE AMERICA MANDALA

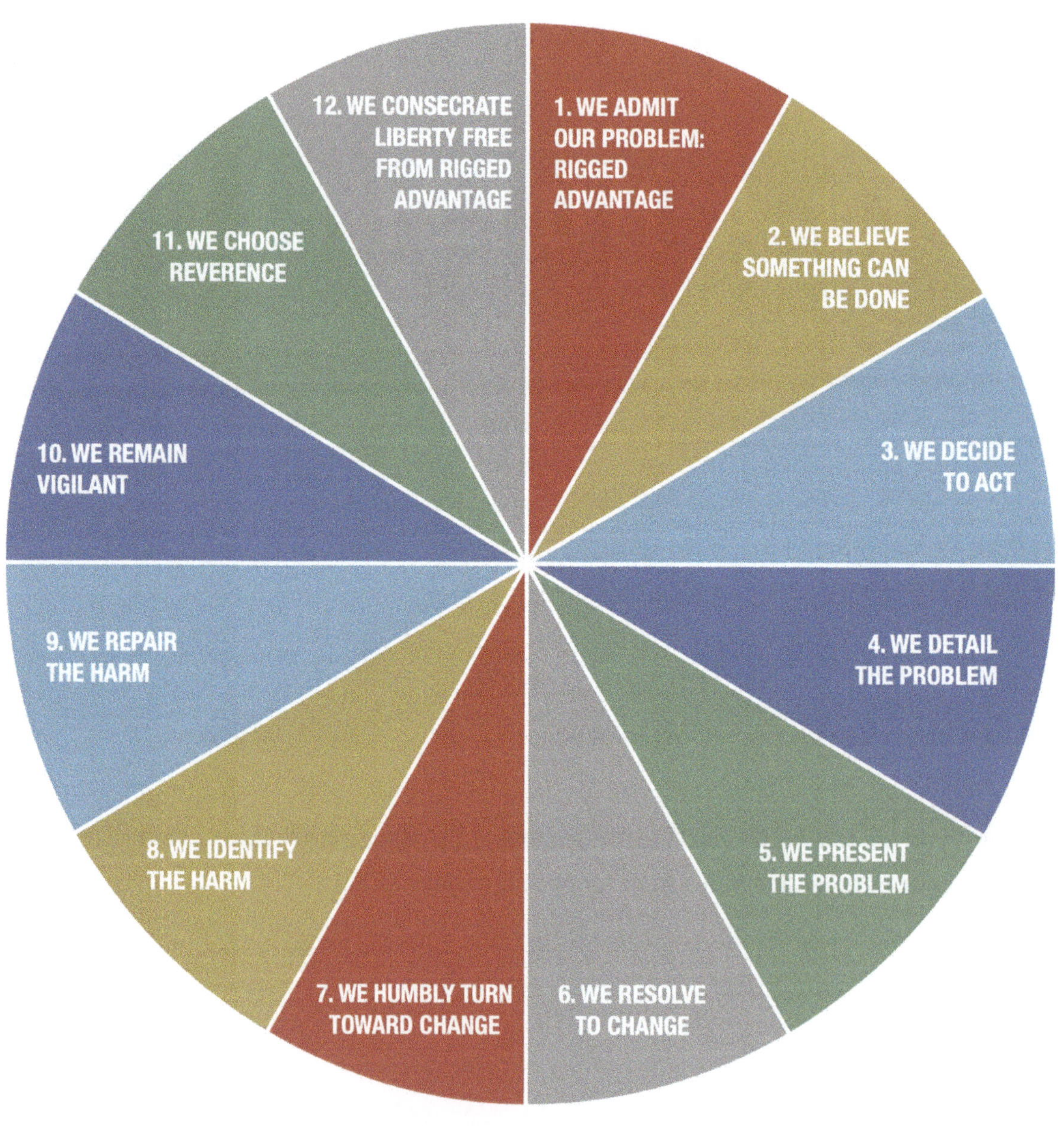

LEARNING OUTCOMES FOR *TWELVE STEPS FOR WHITE AMERICA*

Each step includes a learning outcome, which sets expectations as you learn and practice. Refer to the learning outcomes as you begin working on a step and then again afterward to gauge your progress.

STEP 1 We Admit Our Problem: Rigged Advantage	**STEP 1 LEARNING OUTCOME** Identify the gap between presented and realized democracy in the USA.
STEP 2 We Believe Something Can Be Done	**STEP 2 LEARNING OUTCOME** Recognize the potential for personally impacting democracy's promise.
STEP 3 We Decide to Act	**STEP 3 LEARNING OUTCOME** Determine the need for a personal program of liberation for the common good.
STEP 4 We Detail the Problem	**STEP 4 LEARNING OUTCOME** Identify, analyze, and categorize specific knowledge, skills, and abilities rooted in whiteness-affiliated rigged advantage.

TWELVE STEPS FOR WHITE AMERICA

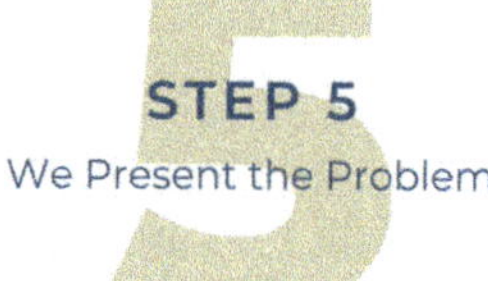

STEP 5

We Present the Problem

STEP 6

We Resolve to Change

STEP 7

We Humbly Turn Toward Change

STEP 8

We Identify the Harm

STEP 5 LEARNING OUTCOME

Recognize, describe, and present specific knowledge, skills, and abilities rooted in whiteness-affiliated rigged advantage.

STEP 6 LEARNING OUTCOME

Contrast intentional vs unintentional beliefs and behaviors that reproduce rigged advantage, then dedicate self to a merit-rich democracy.

STEP 7 LEARNING OUTCOME

Relinquish whiteness-affiliated rigged advantage to habituate justice then liberty for all.

STEP 8 LEARNING OUTCOME

For peace and prosperity, formulate remedies that eliminate disparities in socio-economic outcomes.

TWELVE STEPS FOR WHITE AMERICA

STEP 9
We Repair the Harm

STEP 10
We Remain Vigilant

STEP 11
We Choose Reverence

STEP 12
We Consecrate Liberty Free From Rigged Advantage

TWELVE STEPS FOR WHITE AMERICA

STEP 9 LEARNING OUTCOME
For peace and prosperity, implement remedies that eliminate disparities in socio-economic outcomes.

STEP 10 LEARNING OUTCOME
Habituate rigorous self-assessment to sustain justice then liberty, replacing periodic remission of rigged advantage with its eradication.

STEP 11 LEARNING OUTCOME
Synthesize personal spiritual discipline as the pathway to relinquish rigged advantage for the common good.

STEP 12 LEARNING OUTCOME
Dismantle rigged advantage for an integral democracy where competition thrives from race-neutral merit.

TWELVE STEPS FOR WHITE AMERICA

LEARNING OUTCOMES/INITIAL REVIEW

Make a quick note of your first impressions of the learning outcomes.

Use these first impressions to

- note where you may need concentration or additional support,
- provide a benchmark you can use later to assess how much you have learned, and
- determine after the initial study how you may wish to rewrite the outcome for yourself.

There are no "correct answers" since your impressions are your own.

- What questions do you have? Is there something you don't understand?
- What confronts you? What piques your interest? What sounds right?
- What makes you hopeful for your growth?
- What makes you hopeful for our nation's growth?

LEARNING OUTCOMES: FIRST IMPRESSIONS
1.
2.
3.
4.
5.
6.
7.
8.
9.
10.
11.
12.

PRACTICE MANDALA

Learn the steps well enough to recall them from memory. You need to know the steps to practice them.

As you learn the 12 steps, it may be helpful to use the blank practice mandala provided.

Imagine that the Mandala represents a 12-sided pavilion in a park.

Walk up the steps into the pavilion and stand in Governing Step 1.

Recite governing step 1. Look across the pavilion and recite complementary step 7. Repeat this process for each governing and complementary pair until you have stood in each of the 12 sides.

If you have a 12-member group, form a circle with each of you representing a step.

Recite and discuss each pair.

GOVERNING AND COMPLEMENTARY STEPS

Steps 1–6 each govern complementary steps 7–12. Each complementary step is enabled or limited by the proficiency of its governing step. Looking at the graphic, start at the left with 1 over 7.

Common wisdom says that taking the first step on any journey is the hardest or the most important. Solutions to any problem would have never happened without that first step of exploration. How well you grapple with the first step sets the parameters for all to follow. Some alcoholics talk about "hitting bottom." Unless you are thoroughly convinced there is a problem, you are not ready to work the next steps.

Look at the graphic and ask yourself, "In what way does the complementary step rely on its governing step?"

For example, one will hardly humbly turn toward change (step 7) to solve a problem that they haven't admitted exists (step 1).

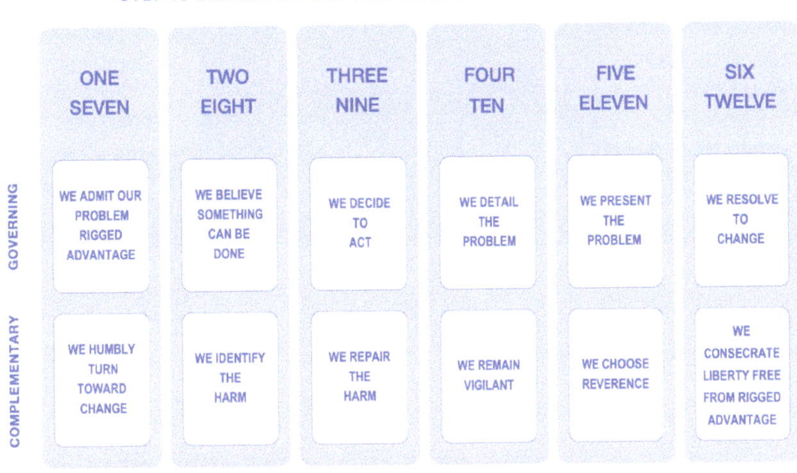

CREATING A FRAMEWORK OF UNDERSTANDING

ELEMENTS IN COMMON

ALCOHOLISM & RIGGED ADVANTAGE

BIO-PSYCHO-SOCIAL DYSFUNCTIONS USE DENIAL & JUSTIFICATION TO DESTROY THE HOST

WRECKAGE OF THE PAST BURDENS THE FUTURE

REMISSION IS WEAK AGAINST STATUS QUO

DWINDLING RELATIONSHIPS COMPENSATE FOR DECLINING CAPACITY

"*SOLUTION*" (DRINKING & SLAVERY ECONOMY) BECAME THE PROBLEM

GENERATIONAL TRANSMISSION OF ENTRENCHED NORMS DIFFICULT TO DISRUPT

COLLUDING CODEPENDENTS MARGINALIZE NON-COLLUDING OTHERS

CONTROL, SCAPEGOAT "OTHERS" WHEN SELF-CONTROL IS PRECARIOUS

TWELVE STEPS FOR WHITE AMERICA #12SWA WWW.WILLIAMWATSON.ORG

National Dysfunction: Not New

Our nation feels so dysfunctional because technology accelerates and permeates across all society what was formerly managed covertly and compartmentally within the norm of rigged advantage. While the extent of this permeating *process* is a new phenomenon, the *content* is not new.

Where and *how much* and *against whom* are new.

White Americans are becoming more aware of how rigged advantage threatens them. "White cold = Black flu" is no longer contained within the norm of rigged advantage. As the pandemic has made abundantly clear, something that affects some of us, can surely affect all of us.

White Americans are increasingly aware that not only Black, Indigenous, and other People of Color pay the price for rigged advantage (which relies on White supremacy and anti-Blackness). Too many White Americans, just trying to make ends meet, trust power White elites who scapegoat "others" as the real problem. Exploited and bamboozled, that trust is killing us—"deaths of despair" at alarming rates. The work of #12SWA is not something we need to do for "others." We need to save "us" so that a *United* States of America—for all—can thrive in a secure and competitive future. Burning down our house does not work.

Tipping Point of Resolve: New

Now that our national dysfunction is "overwhelmingly in our (meaning White America's) face" there is an increasing urgency that something must be done about it. We then realize that "it" has been overwhelmingly in the face of Black America all along. A sufficient tipping point is that we need to understand the problem to change it. As the middle class continues to shrink and the next generation is compromised, more White Americans realize that the membership they pay for Whiteness is too great. Rigged advantage for some = bad for all. It is not just bad for "others."

GOOD NEWS!

Scaffolding illustrates that the dysfunctions of alcoholism and rigged advantage have problem-solving principles in common. We have the skills we need! We just need to apply them to a different problem. That is the point of #12SWA.

SCAFFOLDING

House painters may use scaffolding to extend their reach. Painters do not need to relearn how to paint every time there is a new project with out-of-reach areas. They just need to apply their ability to paint in a new setting using scaffolding. When it comes to learning the *Twelve Steps for White America,* we already have the mastery needed to work these steps. We already apply this mastery in everyday situations.

The Skills Needed for *Twelve Steps for White America* Comprise a Skill Set You Already Have. To Test This, Practice With the Problem of Dirty Dishes.

EVERYDAY PROBLEM-SOLVING PROCESS	MUNDANE APPLICATION
There is a problem.	1. The dishes are dirty.
Something can be done about the problem.	2. The dishes can be cleaned if I put them in the dishwasher.
I want something to be done about the problem.	3. I will put the dishes in the dishwasher.
What exactly is the problem?	4. Leaving the dishes out overnight can create more problems (odor, insects, dried food harder to remove).
Okay. Got it. This is a problem.	5. I acknowledge this is a problem.
Now that I get it, I choose to change it.	6. I'm ready to change this habit.
I want to replace the old behavior with the new.	7. I commit to finally changing this habit.

(*Continued*)

EVERYDAY PROBLEM-SOLVING PROCESS	MUNDANE APPLICATION
Others have been impacted.	8. My spouse or roommate is so tired of me doing this.
Here's how I will fix it.	9. My amends will be to stick to the changed behavior.
Don't slip back into old ways.	10. I'll watch for slipping back into the old habit.
I'm grateful for this change.	11. It feels pretty good taking charge of what I want.
I can change other things and help anyone else if needed!	12. If I can apply this to other needed changes, I will.

Aren't the legacies of slavery a more difficult problem than the problem of dirty dishes? Of course. Let us scaffold to a deadly hard-to-defeat problem, alcoholism.

The Skills Needed for *Twelve Steps for White America* Comprise a Skill Set You Already Have. To Test This, Practice With the Problem of Alcoholism

EVERYDAY PROBLEM-SOLVING PROCESS	APPLICATION FROM ALCOHOLICS ANONYMOUS
There is a problem.	1. We admitted we were powerless over alcohol—that our lives had become unmanageable.
Something can be done about the problem.	2. Came to believe that a power greater than ourselves could restore us to sanity.
I want something to be done about the problem.	3. Made a decision to turn our will and our lives over to the care of God as we understood Him.
What exactly is the problem?	4. Made a searching and fearless moral inventory of ourselves.
Okay. Got it. This is a problem.	5. Admitted to God, to ourselves, and to another human being the exact nature of our wrongs.
Now that I get it, I choose to change it.	6. Were entirely ready to have God remove all these defects of character.
I want to replace the old behavior with the new.	7. Humbly asked Him to remove our shortcomings.

(*Continued*)

EVERYDAY PROBLEM-SOLVING PROCESS	APPLICATION FROM ALCOHOLICS ANONYMOUS
Others have been impacted.	8. Made a list of all persons we had harmed and became willing to make amends to them all.
Here's how I will fix it.	9. Made direct amends to such people wherever possible, except when to do so would injure them or others.
Don't slip back into old ways.	10. Continued to take personal inventory and when we were wrong promptly admitted it.
I'm grateful for this change.	11. Sought through prayer and meditation to improve our conscious contact with God as we understood Him, praying only for knowledge of His will for us and the power to carry that out.
I can change other things and help anyone else if needed!	12. Having had a spiritual awakening as the result of these steps, we tried to carry this message to alcoholics and to practice these principles in all our affairs.

The Skills Needed for *Twelve Steps for White America* Comprise a Skill Set You Already Have. To Test This, Practice With the Problem of Rigged Advantage

EVERYDAY PROBLEM-SOLVING PROCESS	APPLICATION TO RIGGED ADVANTAGE
There is a problem.	1. We admit our problem: rigged advantage.
Something can be done about the problem.	2. We believe something can be done.
I want something to be done about the problem.	3. We decide to act.
What exactly is the problem?	4. We detail the problem.
Okay. Got it. This is a problem.	5. We present the problem.
Now that I get it, I choose to change it.	6. We resolve to change.
I want to replace the old behavior with the new.	7. We humbly turn toward change.
Others have been impacted.	8. We identify the harm.
Here's how I will fix it.	9. We repair the harm.

(*Continued*)

EVERYDAY PROBLEM-SOLVING PROCESS	APPLICATION TO RIGGED ADVANTAGE
Don't slip back into old ways.	10. We remain vigilant.
I'm grateful for this change.	11. We choose reverence.
I can change other things and help anyone else if needed!	12. We consecrate liberty free from rigged advantage.

You already have the skills to address rigged advantage, because you use these skills every day. The 12 steps provide you with an opportunity for a personal program of practice, ultimately for your own benefit, for your growth and liberation.

If enough Americans practiced these steps, a tipping point of citizenship would strengthen our fragile American experiment with democracy. Our best days could be ahead of us.

RIGGED ADVANTAGE GRAPHIC AND NUTSHELL

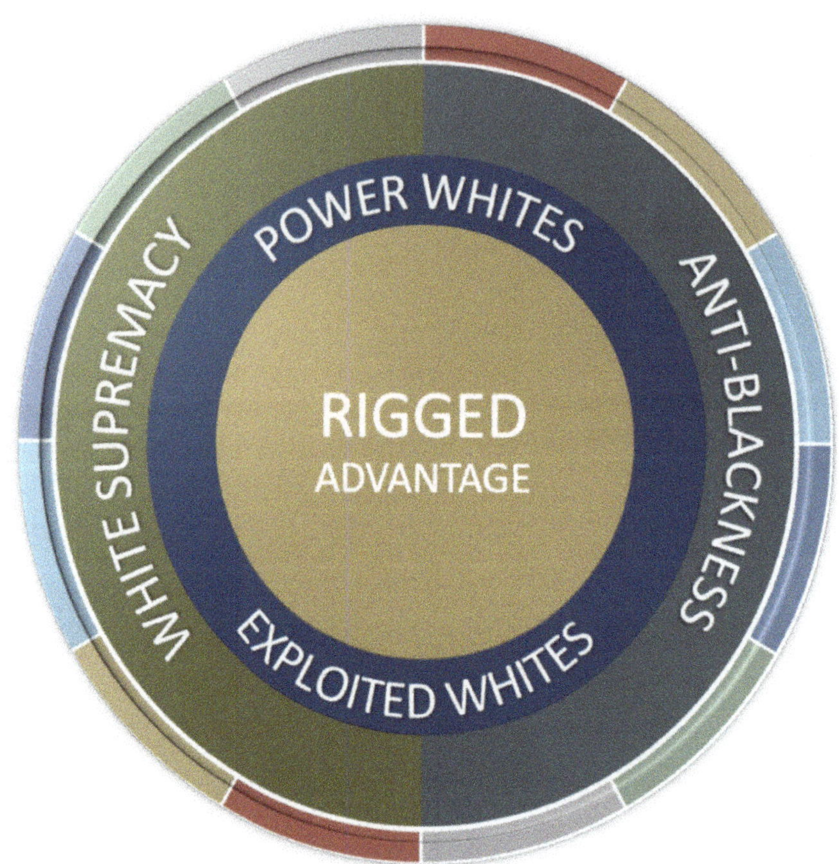

Power whites rig advantage using Whiteness to co-opt exploited Whites' affinity in exchange for derivative and tenuous value embedded in social constructs of race.[1]

Whiteness masquerades as solidarity while masking within-group exploitation.

1 Allen, T. (2012a). *The invention of the White race: Racial oppression and social control* (Vol. 1). Verso; Allen, T. (2012b). *The invention of the White race: Racial oppression and social control* (Vol. 2). Verso.

The delusional mechanism[2] enabling exploited Whites to experience the value[3] of Whiteness versus their subjective exploitation[4] persists through two strategies:

- White supremacy (n.): Social reinforcements that disproportionately value Whiteness.
- Anti-Blackness (v.): Displace exploitation onto Black, Indigenous, and other People of Color.

White supremacy and Anti-Blackness strategy mechanisms include racelighting,[5] voter suppression, minority rule, state-sanctioned violence, disproportionate incarceration, disparate outcomes in education, generational wealth, health, economic-social mobility.

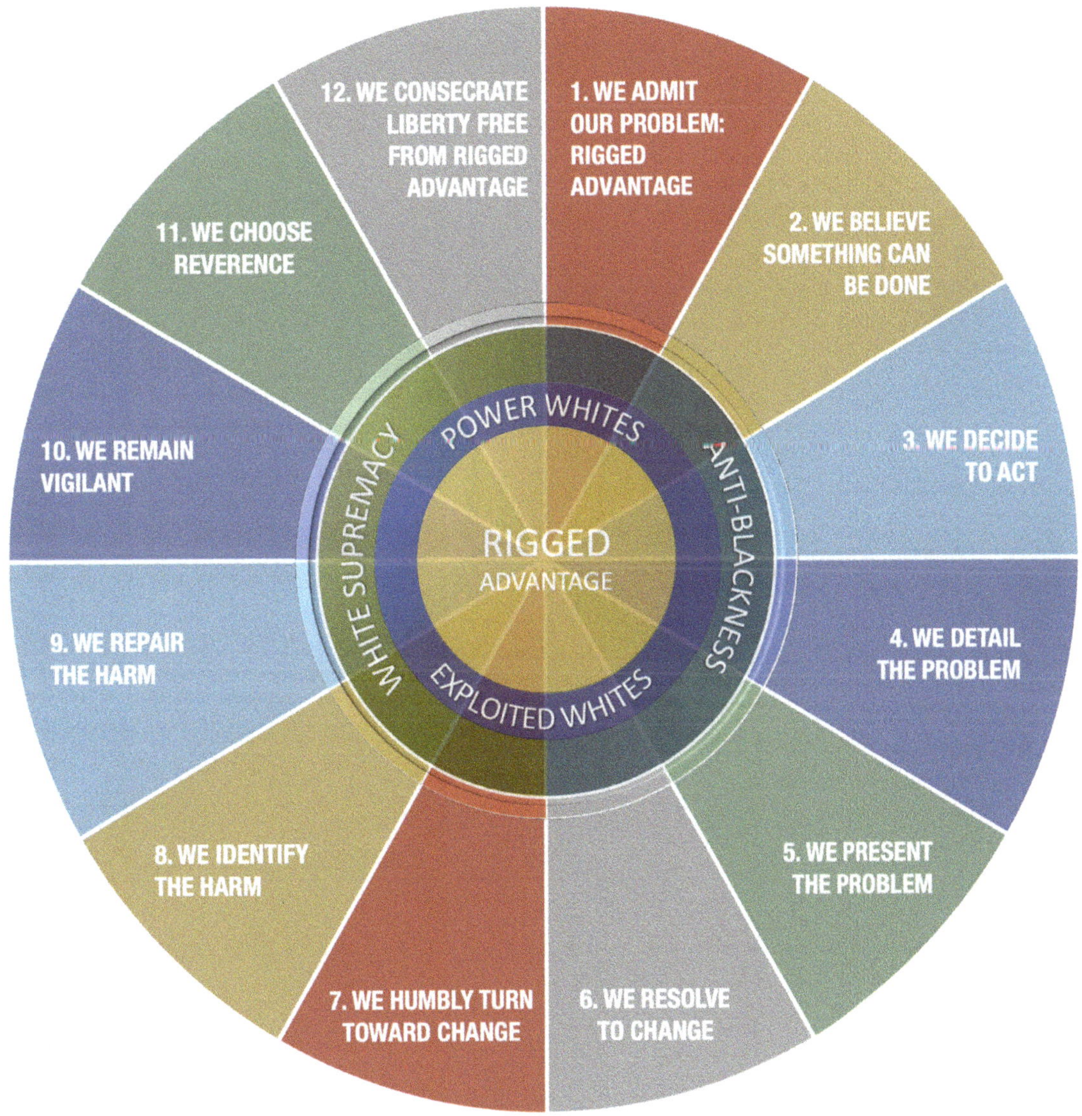

2 Stoute, B. J. (2017). Race and racism in psychoanalytic thought: The ghosts in our nursery. *The American Psychoanalyst*, 51(1). https://apsa.org/apsaa-publications/vol51no1-TOC/html/vol51no1_08.xhtml
3 Glaude, E. S., Jr. (2017). *Democracy in Black: How race still enslaves the American soul.* Broadway Books.
4 Deranty, J. P. (2016). Exploited: Exploitation as a subjective category. *The Southern Journal of Philosophy, 54*(S1), 31–43. https://doi.org/10.1111/sjp.12185
5 Harris, F., III, & Wood, J. L. (2021, February 12). Racelighting: A prevalent version of gaslighting facing People of Color. *Diverse: Issues in Higher Education*. https://www.diverseeducation.com/opinion/article/15108651/racelighting-a-prevalent-version-of-gaslighting-facing-people-of-color

Practice Rigged Advantage: Two Sides of the Same Whiteness Coin

An Exercise Module for Critical Thinking, Discernment, Focus, Perspective

(Refer to the next page).

CRITICAL THINKING

The module "Rigged Advantage: Two Sides of the Same Whiteness Coin" is intended to provoke your thinking.

Someone is sure to "be offended."
Being offended is easy.
Critical thinking is hard!

DISCERNMENT

What is required for democracy is intellectual discernment. Practice thinking for yourself. Knee-jerk reactions contribute very little to democracy except for "unrest," which is the fodder of manipulators who rely on your distraction to get and keep what they want.

FOCUS

Assert your authority to manage how you experience information. Imagine this exercise as the subject of a debate team. Debate teams learn to master the art of constructing, presenting, and defending or opposing an argument.

PERSPECTIVE

Your job as a member of this debate team is to argue for and argue against. Doing this will ensure that you cultivate mastery over perspective.

Write your notes for the argument.

Write your notes against the argument.

Rigged Advantage: Two Sides of the Same Coin

Power Whites bamboozle* exploited Whites to advance a power White agenda using *Otherness*.[6] (We are valued[7] White Americans and not Others; i.e., devalued Black Americans). White supremacy ensures that exploited Whites abhor Otherness (anti-Blackness) and vote against exploited Whites' self-interest to sustain power White advantage. If exploited Whites withdrew from the Whiteness political coalition to vote with other exploited groups, the power White status quo would erode.

- *Bamboozling is a time-worn technique alive and well in the 21st century.
- "Bamboozle" is an 18th-century term for self gain through exploiting others with deceit and trickery.
- Its meaning was extended in the 19th century by the context of Jim Crow minstrelsy: anti-Blackness as entertainment.
- The 20th-century version of bamboozling presented as distraction, disinformation, scapegoating, voter suppression, and brutality.
- In the 21st century, social media propagates bamboozling: Echo chambers congeal contorted seemingly unmatched coalitions.
- Minority rule in government perpetuates plantation control over the many by the few to sustain the status quo for power Whites.

<table>
<tr><td rowspan="2">Case Example of Whiteness in the United States of America</td><td>IMG 0.14a  </td><td>IMG 0.14b  </td><td rowspan="2">Two sides of the same Whiteness coin glued together with white supremacy for rigged advantage.</td></tr>
<tr><td>SIDE A: POWER WHITES
• CA: 40 million people = 2 senators
• Fifth largest economy in the world
• San José and San Francisco are bastions of inequality in the United States</td><td>SIDE B: EXPLOITED WHITES
• MS: 3 million people = 2 senators
• 96th largest economy in the world (behind Morocco)
• MS consistently ranks near or at the bottom of socioeconomic indicators in the United States</td></tr>
</table>

As the epicenter of American inequality, San José and San Francisco lead a democracy-threatening transfer of wealth to the very few at the top. Their stellar reputations for being diverse liberal bastions mask how they sustain rigged advantage for power White America. While California's 40 million people have two senators, Mississippi's two senators, representing 3 million people (less than 1/10th of California's 40 million people), consistently vote for power White advantage, even when their own people languish exploited like millions of Californians.

How is this possible?

Two sides of the same Whiteness coin are glued together through White supremacy to rig advantage. This answer is important to understanding the steps White Americans need to take for American democracy. Exploited Whites vote with power Whites because of bamboozled convictions (race habits[8]) habituated in the sticks and carrots of racism.

The stick: Avoid anti-Blackness: "I may not be rich, but I am White—not one of those subjected and de-valued others."

The carrot: Reap the benefits of White privilege: "I may not be rich, but I am White. This land was made for me."

It serves power Whites that California stereotypes Mississippi for its "Southern racism." In truth, a slight realignment of Whiteness affinity in Mississippi (largest Black American population in the United States) could help save America from California.

6 powell, j. a. (2015). *Racing to justice: Transforming our conceptions of self and other to build an inclusive society.* Indiana University Press.
7 Glaude (2017).
8 Glaude (2017).

RIGGED ADVANTAGE POINTS FOR DISCUSSION

Suggested Points for Discussion

Rigged advantage is a self-reinforcing entitlement where power Whites exploit other Whites in a collusion of Whiteness. Power Whites rely on exploited Whites to displace their experience of subjective exploitation using White supremacy and anti-Blackness.

Transferred across generations into the present, displaced exploitation was prototyped onto enslaved others who were power Whites' property and Native Americans who were power Whites' conquest. This rigged advantage surges now as increased inequality.* The greater the inequality, the greater the extremes of Othering.

Increasing inequality in the United States is concerning on its own, but it coincides with a growing proliferation of information echo chambers and media consolidations, which creates profit for some power Whites, and creates benefit for all power Whites.

Echo chambers and media conglomerates falsely present as sources of information vital to democracy. However, because they are beholden to shareholder value, they exploit consumer urges for worldview coherence.

The Whiteness voting block (relies on minority rule) sustains rigged advantage for power Whites, while it exploits other Whites. If exploited Whites chose to vote with others versus against their self-interests, status quo benefit for power Whites would erode.

Create Your Own Additional Points for Discussion

DRAW THE CIRCLE

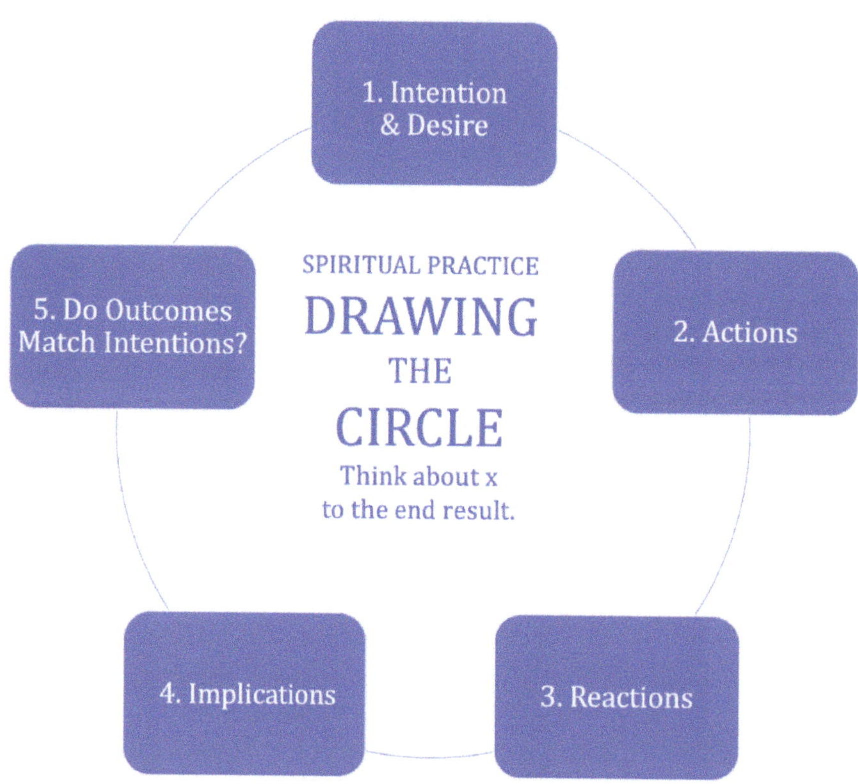

Practice "Drawing the Circle" for Any Given Principled Position You May Hold. Repeat Often

1. What is your intention and desire?

   ____

   ____

2. What actions have you or others initiated that reflect your intention?

   ____

   ____

3. What reactions/consequences have been generated as a result?

   ____

   ____

4. What are the implications of these reactions? *Be rigorously honest. Your preconceived notions may be insufficient to answer this question. That means you will need to seek out research-based information to challenge your capability.*

   ____

   ____

5. Do the results of these reactions match what you intended?

   ____

   ____

Image Credits

IMG 0.14a: Copyright © 2014 Depositphotos/Mertsalovvw.

IMG 0.15a: Copyright © 2014 Depositphotos/Mertsalovvw.

PART I

STEPS 1–4: UNSHACKLE THE PAST

TRUTH

REPENTANCE

STOP AND TURN

Introduction to Part I

1. We admit there is a problem.
2. We believe something can be done about the problem.
3. We decide to do something about the problem.
4. We get specific about the details of the problem.

These are the problem-solving steps we take every day. We apply these steps to both the complex and the mundane. Throughout our lives, the *content* of problems differs, but the *process* of problem solving has elements in common. The process is repeatable in languages across the human condition.
We already know *how* to do what needs to be done for a United States of America.
We already know a great deal of *what* needs to be done.
Part of the problem and part of the solution is already manifest within us.
Each of us has a part to play:

- whether we intend anything or we do not,
- whether we have given it a second thought, or
- whether it concerns us at all.

We start by telling the truth. Then, we stop and turn from (known since ancient history as repentance) what does not work toward what works. We cut ties to what does not work to capitalize on what works and manage the risk of unnecessary repetition, which threatens evolving progress.
For the problem of cutting ties to rigged advantage in a divided United States, I deliberately use the potent and painful language that we must unshackle the past.

Part I prepares us to cut these ties.
Cutting the ties comes later, but for now, we take this one step at a time.

This is very simple:
Tell the truth (be honest).
Stop, turn (quit doing it).
Unshackle the past (release it).
This is very simple, but it *is not* easy, is it?
While it may not be easy, it truly *is not complicated*.

1. WE ADMIT OUR PROBLEM: RIGGED ADVANTAGE

7. WE HUMBLY TURN TOWARD CHANGE

How does the author compare alcoholism to rigged advantage?

Why is the first step "the hardest"?

COMPLETE ANY SECTION AS YOU ARE READY. BE CONCISE. REVIEW AS YOU PROGRESS.		
WHAT IS STEP 1? SAY IT AS YOU WRITE IT.	WHAT IS THE LEARNING OUTCOME FOR STEP 1?	WHAT ARE KEY WORDS FROM STEP 1?
STEP 1 GOVERNS STEP 7. WHAT MUST OCCUR IN STEP 1 FOR STEP 7 LATER?	WHAT ARE YOU LEARNING?	WHAT DOES DEMOCRACY REQUIRE? WHO DO YOU WANT TO BE? WHAT IS YOUR PLAN?

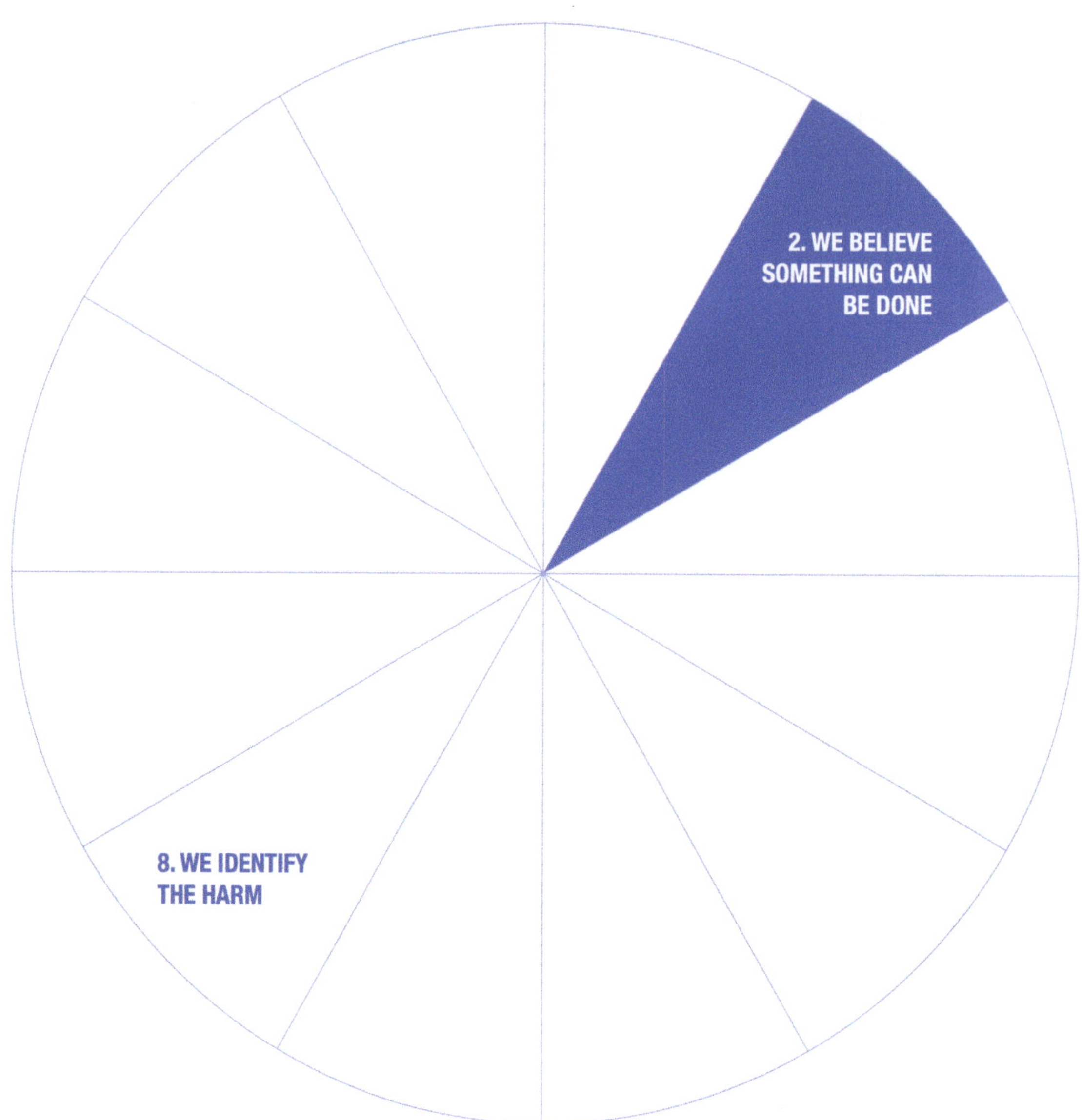

Why does believing something can be done matter when addressing problems?

How do norms enable us to "not see" a problem others can readily identify?

COMPLETE ANY SECTION AS YOU ARE READY. BE CONCISE. REVIEW AS YOU PROGRESS.		
WHAT IS STEP 2? SAY IT AS YOU WRITE IT.	WHAT IS THE LEARNING OUTCOME FOR STEP 2?	WHAT ARE KEY WORDS FROM STEP 2?
STEP 2 GOVERNS STEP 8. WHAT MUST OCCUR IN STEP 2 FOR STEP 8 LATER?	WHAT ARE YOU LEARNING?	WHAT DOES DEMOCRACY REQUIRE? WHO DO YOU WANT TO BE? WHAT IS YOUR PLAN?

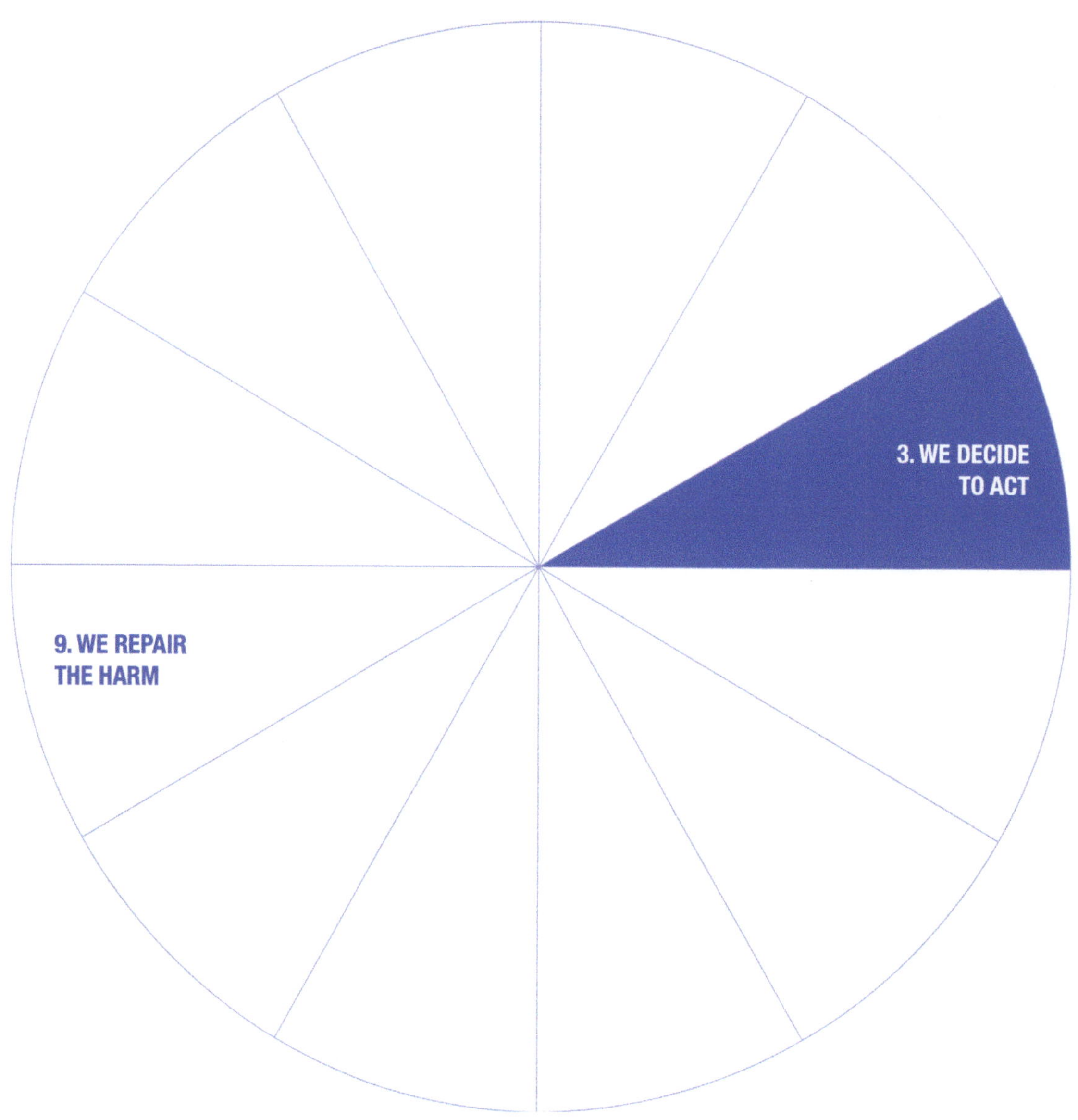

Our will cements bad habits and good habits. What is the power of making a decision?

Describe a situation where you resisted making changes even after you knew they were needed.

COMPLETE ANY SECTION AS YOU ARE READY. BE CONCISE. REVIEW AS YOU PROGRESS.		
WHAT IS STEP 3? SAY IT AS YOU WRITE IT.	WHAT IS THE LEARNING OUTCOME FOR STEP 3?	WHAT ARE KEY WORDS FROM STEP 3?
STEP 3 GOVERNS STEP 9. WHAT MUST OCCUR IN STEP 3 FOR STEP 9 LATER?	WHAT ARE YOU LEARNING?	WHAT DOES DEMOCRACY REQUIRE? WHO DO YOU WANT TO BE? WHAT IS YOUR PLAN?

(See the step 4 appendix for the contextualized family history assessment.)

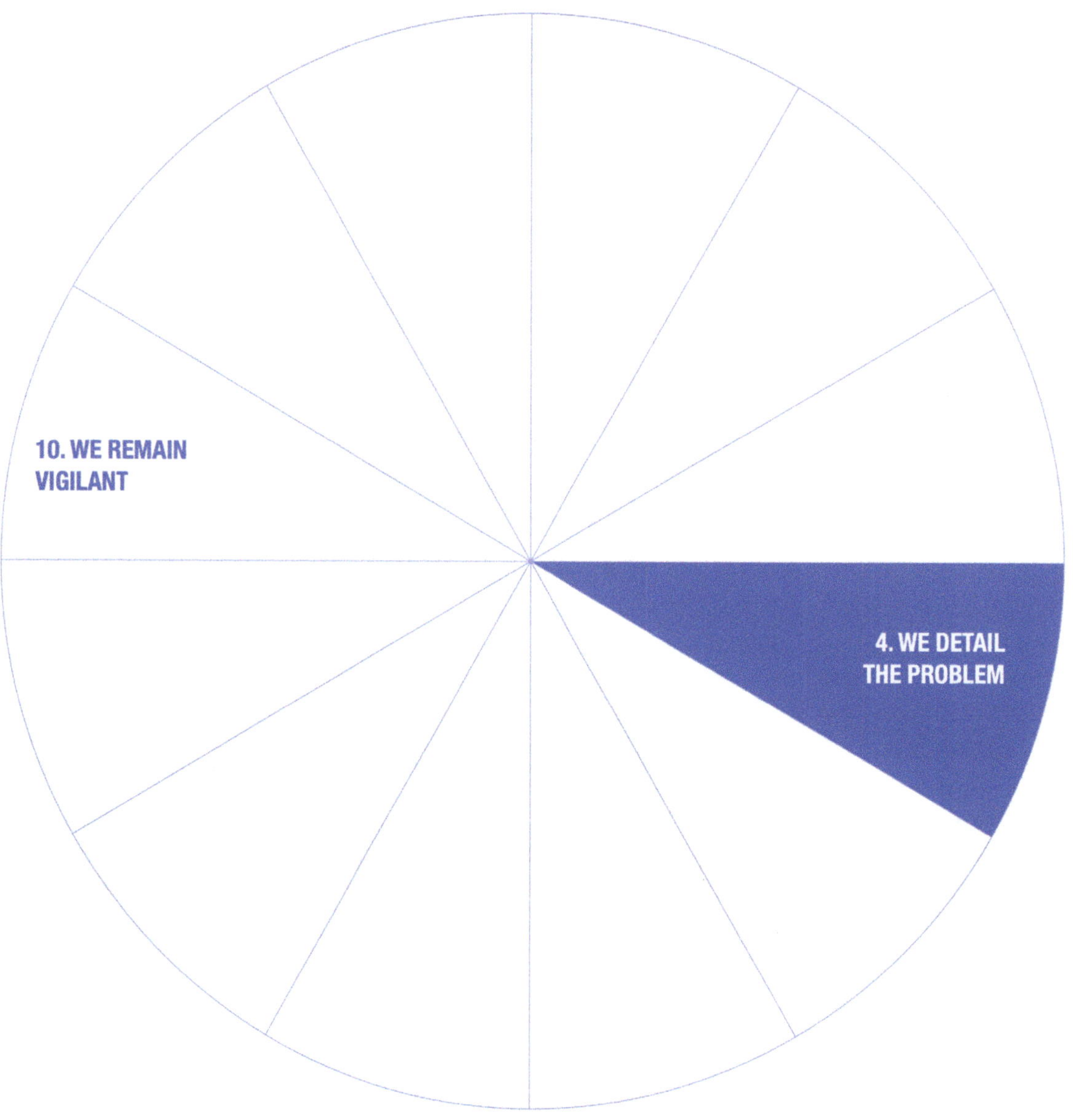

How does getting specific about a problem facilitate change?

How can rationalizing behavior leave problems dormant for the future?

COMPLETE ANY SECTION AS YOU ARE READY. BE CONCISE. REVIEW AS YOU PROGRESS.		
COMPLETE THE CONTEXTUALIZED FAMILY HISTORY ASSESSMENT, THE APPENDIX FOR STEP 4.		
WHAT IS STEP 4? SAY IT AS YOU WRITE IT.	WHAT IS THE LEARNING OUTCOME FOR STEP 4?	WHAT ARE KEY WORDS FROM STEP 4?
STEP 4 GOVERNS STEP 10. WHAT MUST OCCUR IN STEP 4 FOR STEP 10 LATER?	WHAT ARE YOU LEARNING?	WHAT DOES DEMOCRACY REQUIRE? WHO DO YOU WANT TO BE? WHAT IS YOUR PLAN?

PART II

02

RECONCILIATION
ATONEMENT
STRENGTHEN U.S. SECURITY AND GLOBAL COMPETITIVENESS

Intro: Part II Prepares Your Discovery to Venture Outward

PART II: Steps 5–8

EVERYDAY PROBLEM-SOLVING PROCESS	APPLICATION TO RIGGED ADVANTAGE
Okay. Got it. This is a problem.	5. We present the problem.
Now that I get it, I choose to change it.	6. We resolve to change.
I want to replace the old behavior with the new.	7. We humbly turn toward change.
Others have been impacted.	8. We identify the harm.

Steps 5 through 8 build on the inward discovery and establish a pathway outward toward the Other: what we perceive to be separate from "us" both as individuals and the group with which we identify.

Step 5 can be thought of as a confessional, coming clean, getting honest about what you discovered, clarifying or refining ideas by presenting them to others. Presenting authenticates, validates, and reinforces. We come clean. We get it off our chest. We unburden ourselves. A weight is lifted off our shoulders. Confession is good for the soul.

Step 6 is a resolution about what you do now that you have come this far in the process. As we all know from our years of New Year resolutions, a resolution represents an intention—something necessary but insufficient. An intention does not achieve the outcome of the resolve, but there is no result without it.

Step 7 is a getting-started step. Step 7 is a step toward a future now made possible by your progress: (1) truth, (2) belief, (3) will, (4) inventory, (5) expression, (6) resolution, (7) start, (8) account.

Step 8 is where some sobriety arrives and begins for the storm-shelter family we mentioned earlier. Instead of the alcoholic emerging from the storm cellar after a tornado to proclaim "Ain't it grand the wind stopped blowing," the alcoholic has worked the steps sufficiently to ask the question, "Who has been impacted by the wreckage of my stormy life and how?"

Astute readers will notice that we are already over half-way through the steps, and we are still only preparing to do something: to work toward a solution for the problem of rigged advantage.

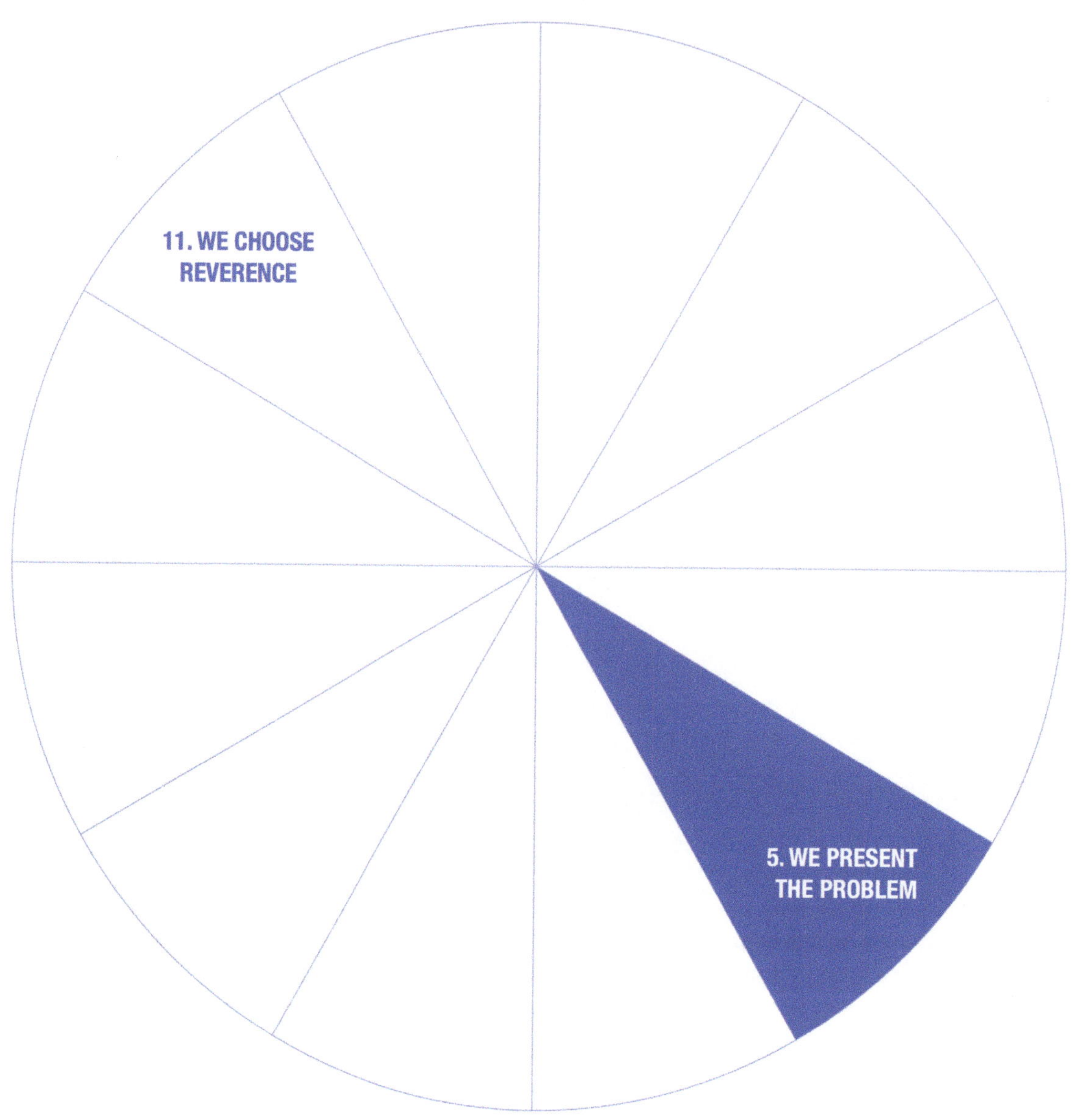

How does describing something to others help you clarify it for yourself?

Why is confession good for the soul?

COMPLETE ANY SECTION AS YOU ARE READY. BE CONCISE. REVIEW AS YOU PROGRESS.		
WHAT IS STEP 5? SAY IT AS YOU WRITE IT.	WHAT IS THE LEARNING OUTCOME FOR STEP 5?	WHAT ARE KEY WORDS FROM STEP 5?
STEP 5 GOVERNS STEP 11. WHAT MUST OCCUR IN STEP 5 FOR STEP 11 LATER?	WHAT ARE YOU LEARNING?	WHAT DOES DEMOCRACY REQUIRE? WHO DO YOU WANT TO BE? WHAT IS YOUR PLAN?

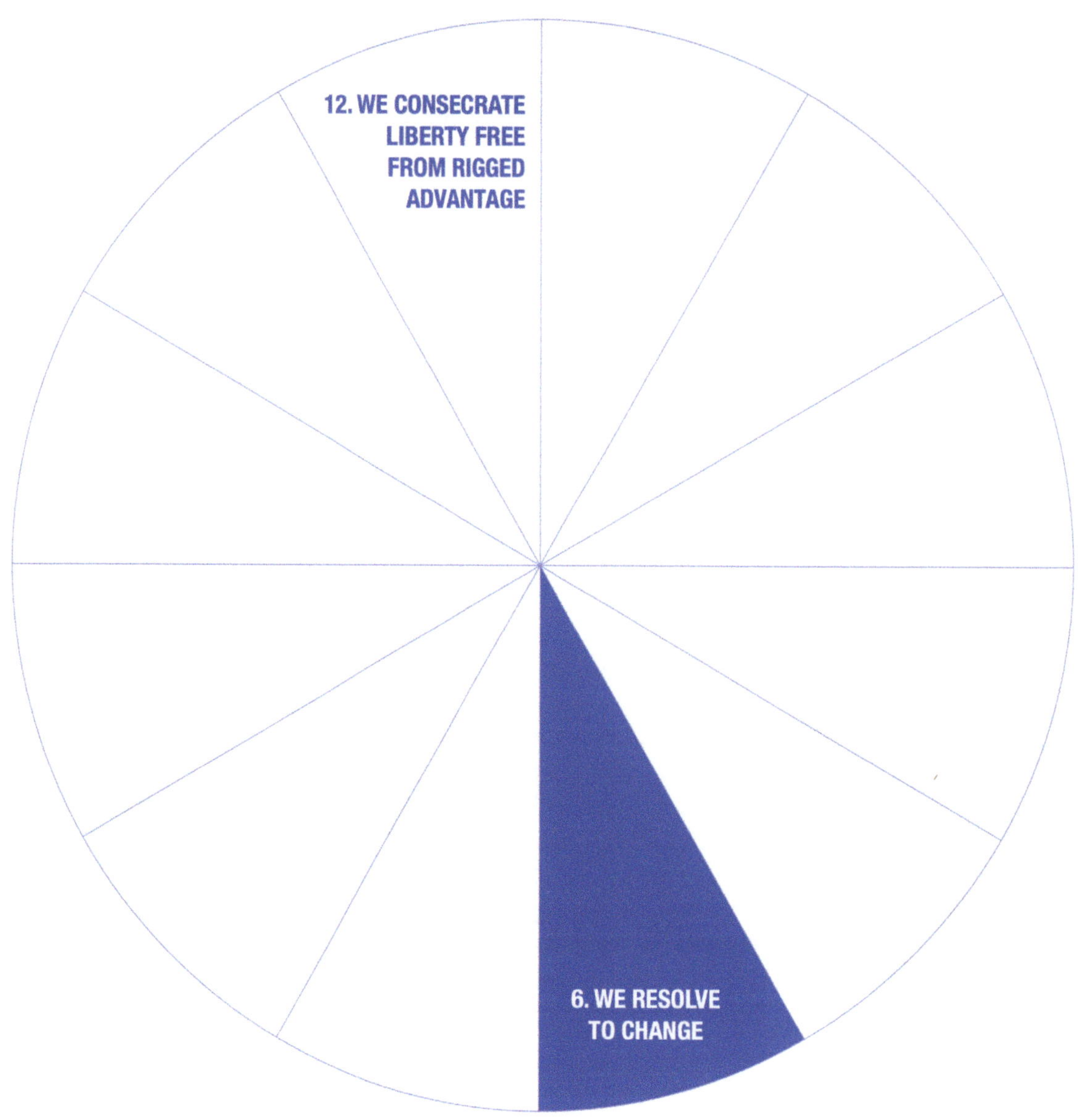

Why is admitting, believing, deciding, clarifying, and reporting not enough for change?

Why is that which we recently learned not as strong as something practiced longer?

COMPLETE ANY SECTION AS YOU ARE READY. BE CONCISE. REVIEW AS YOU PROGRESS.		
WHAT IS STEP 6? SAY IT AS YOU WRITE IT.	WHAT IS THE LEARNING OUTCOME FOR STEP 6?	WHAT ARE KEY WORDS FROM STEP 6?
STEP 6 GOVERNS STEP 12. WHAT MUST OCCUR IN STEP 6 FOR STEP 12 LATER?	WHAT ARE YOU LEARNING?	WHAT DOES DEMOCRACY REQUIRE? WHO DO YOU WANT TO BE? WHAT IS YOUR PLAN?

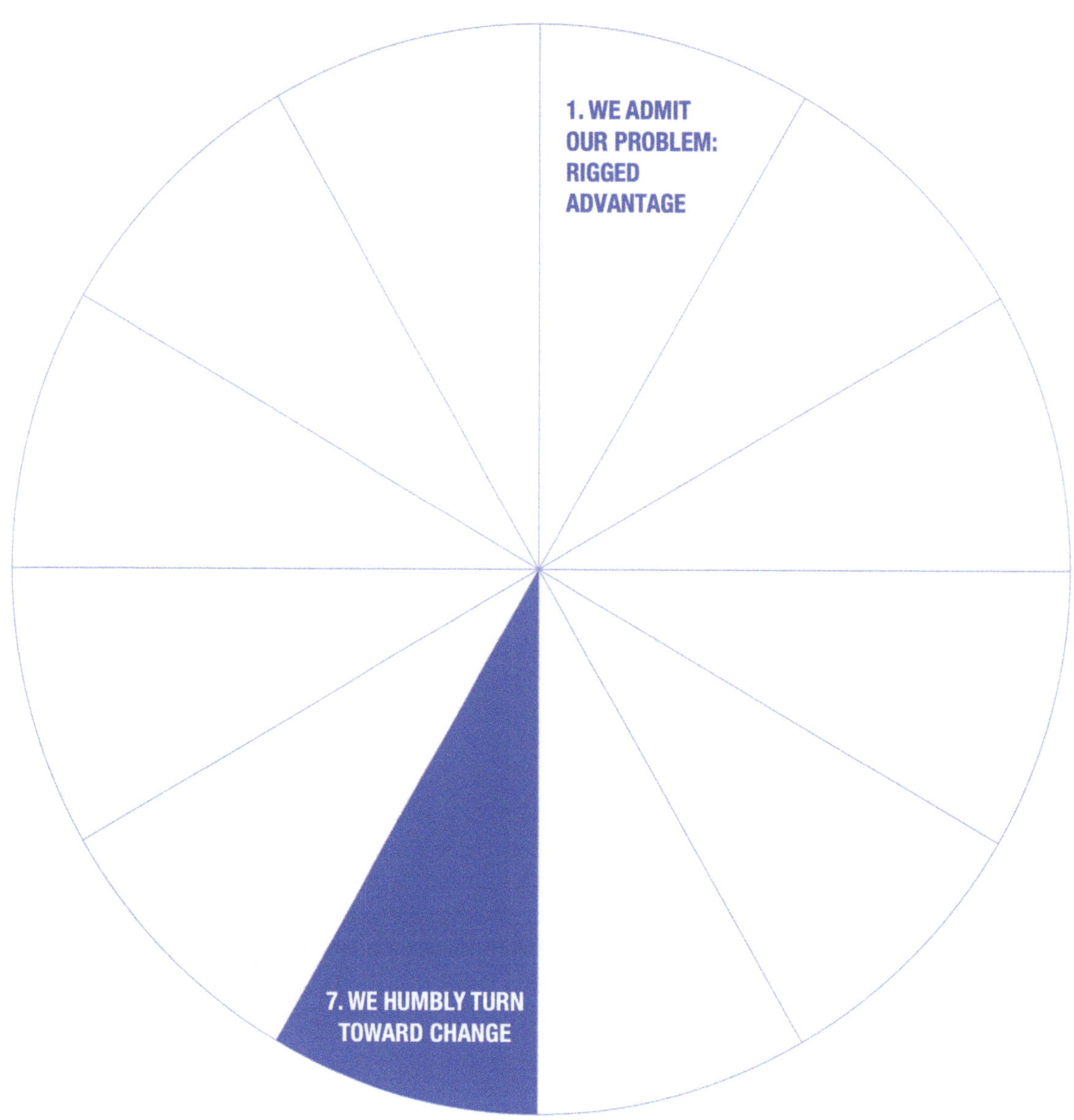

What is the relationship between humility and change?

Humility is contextual. What are examples of how humility improved your life?

COMPLETE ANY SECTION AS YOU ARE READY. BE CONCISE. REVIEW AS YOU PROGRESS.		
WHAT IS STEP 7? SAY IT AS YOU WRITE IT.	WHAT IS THE LEARNING OUTCOME FOR STEP 7?	WHAT ARE KEY WORDS FROM STEP 7 CHAPTER IN THE BOOK?
STEP 7 DEPENDS ON STEP 1. DESCRIBE HOW.	WHAT ARE YOU LEARNING?	WHAT DOES DEMOCRACY REQUIRE? WHO DO YOU WANT TO BE? WHAT IS YOUR PLAN?

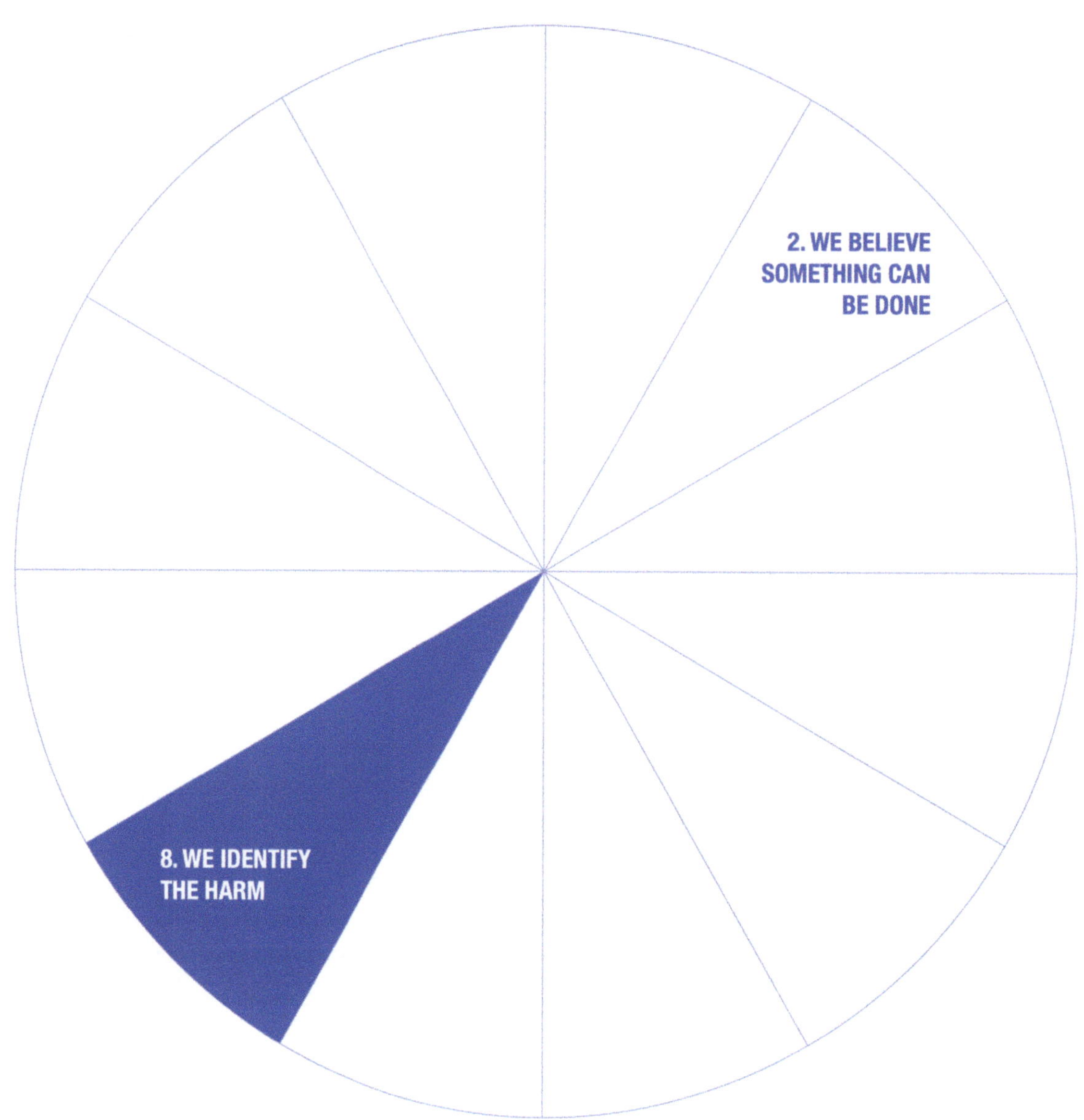

What does the following saying mean? "When we know better, we do better."

How does self-awareness enable us to assess our impact on others?

COMPLETE ANY SECTION AS YOU ARE READY. BE CONCISE. REVIEW AS YOU PROGRESS.		
WHAT IS STEP 8? SAY IT AS YOU WRITE IT.	WHAT IS THE LEARNING OUTCOME FOR STEP 8?	WHAT ARE KEY WORDS FROM STEP 8?
STEP 8 DEPENDS ON STEP 2. DESCRIBE HOW.	WHAT ARE YOU LEARNING?	WHAT DOES DEMOCRACY REQUIRE? WHO DO YOU WANT TO BE? WHAT IS YOUR PLAN?

PART III

STEPS 9–12: MAKE WAY FOR ALL

RENEWAL

REDEMPTION

LIVE DEMOCRACY'S PROMISE

MAKE WAY FOR ALL, SO OUR BEST DAYS ARE AHEAD OF US

Intro: Part III Renewal Makes Way for All—Our Best Days Ahead

PART III: Steps 9–12

EVERYDAY PROBLEM-SOLVING PROCESS	APPLICATION TO RIGGED ADVANTAGE
Here's how I will fix it.	9. We repair the harm.
Don't slip back into old ways.	10. We remain vigilant.
I'm grateful for this change.	11. We choose reverence.
I can change other things and help anyone else if needed!	12. We consecrate liberty free from rigged advantage.

Step 9: We repair the harm

Learning outcome: For peace and prosperity, implement remedies that eliminate disparities in socioeconomic outcomes.

Step 10: We remain vigilant

Learning outcome: Habituate rigorous self-assessment to sustain justice, then liberty, replacing periodic remission of rigged advantage with its eradication.

Step 11: We choose reverence

Learning outcome: Synthesize personal spiritual discipline as the pathway to relinquish rigged advantage for the common good.

Step 12: We consecrate liberty free from rigged advantage

Learning outcome: Dismantle rigged advantage for an integral democracy where competition thrives from race-neutral merit.

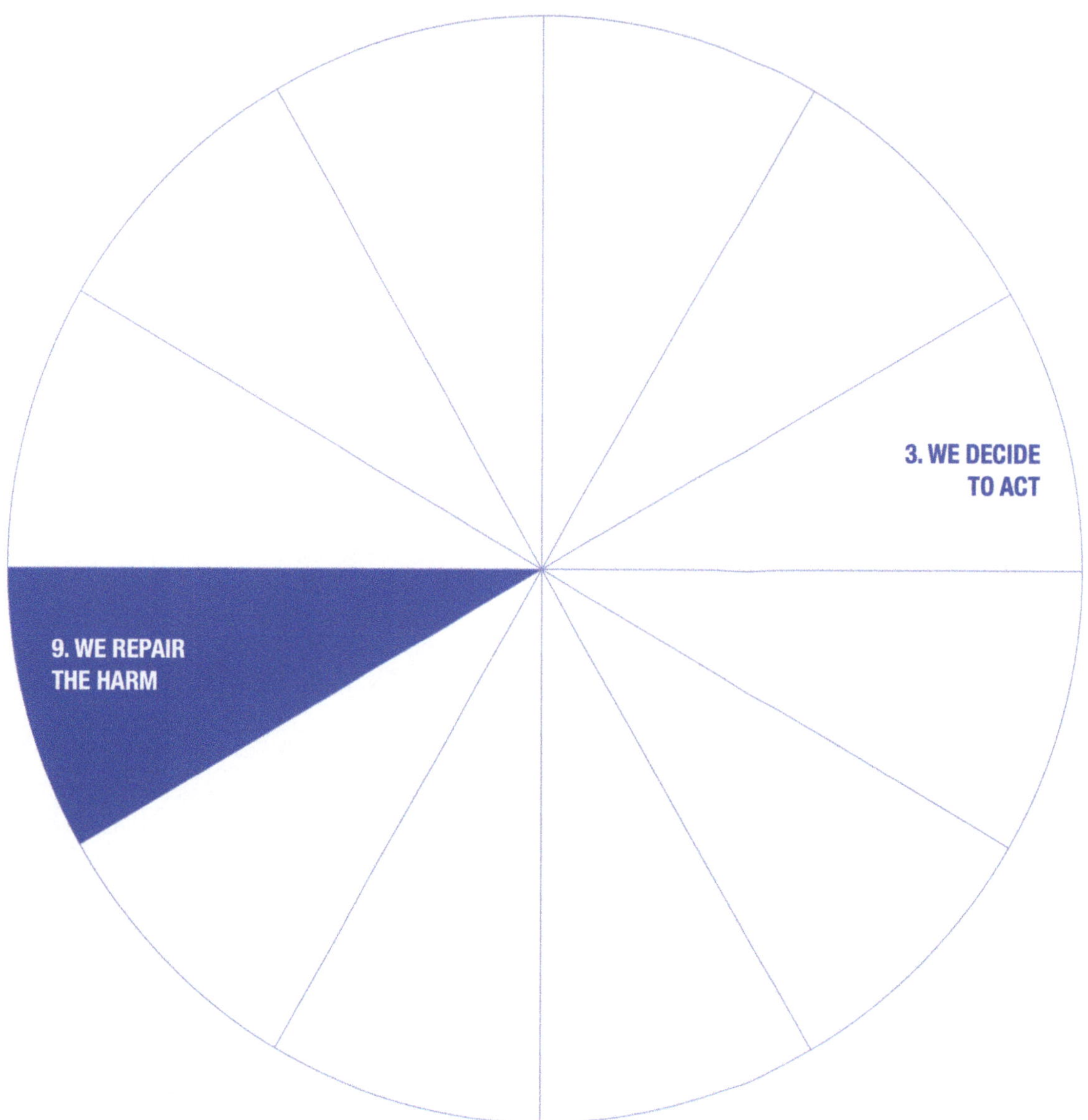

Steps 1–8 are inner work. How is step 9 the first step that serves someone else?

How does knowing that a remedy is needed differ from knowing what the remedy is?

COMPLETE ANY SECTION AS YOU ARE READY. BE CONCISE. REVIEW AS YOU PROGRESS.		
WHAT IS STEP 9? SAY IT AS YOU WRITE IT.	WHAT IS THE LEARNING OUTCOME FOR STEP 9?	WHAT ARE KEY WORDS FROM STEP 9?
STEP 9 DEPENDS ON STEP 3. DESCRIBE HOW.	WHAT ARE YOU LEARNING?	WHAT DOES DEMOCRACY REQUIRE? WHO DO YOU WANT TO BE? WHAT IS YOUR PLAN?

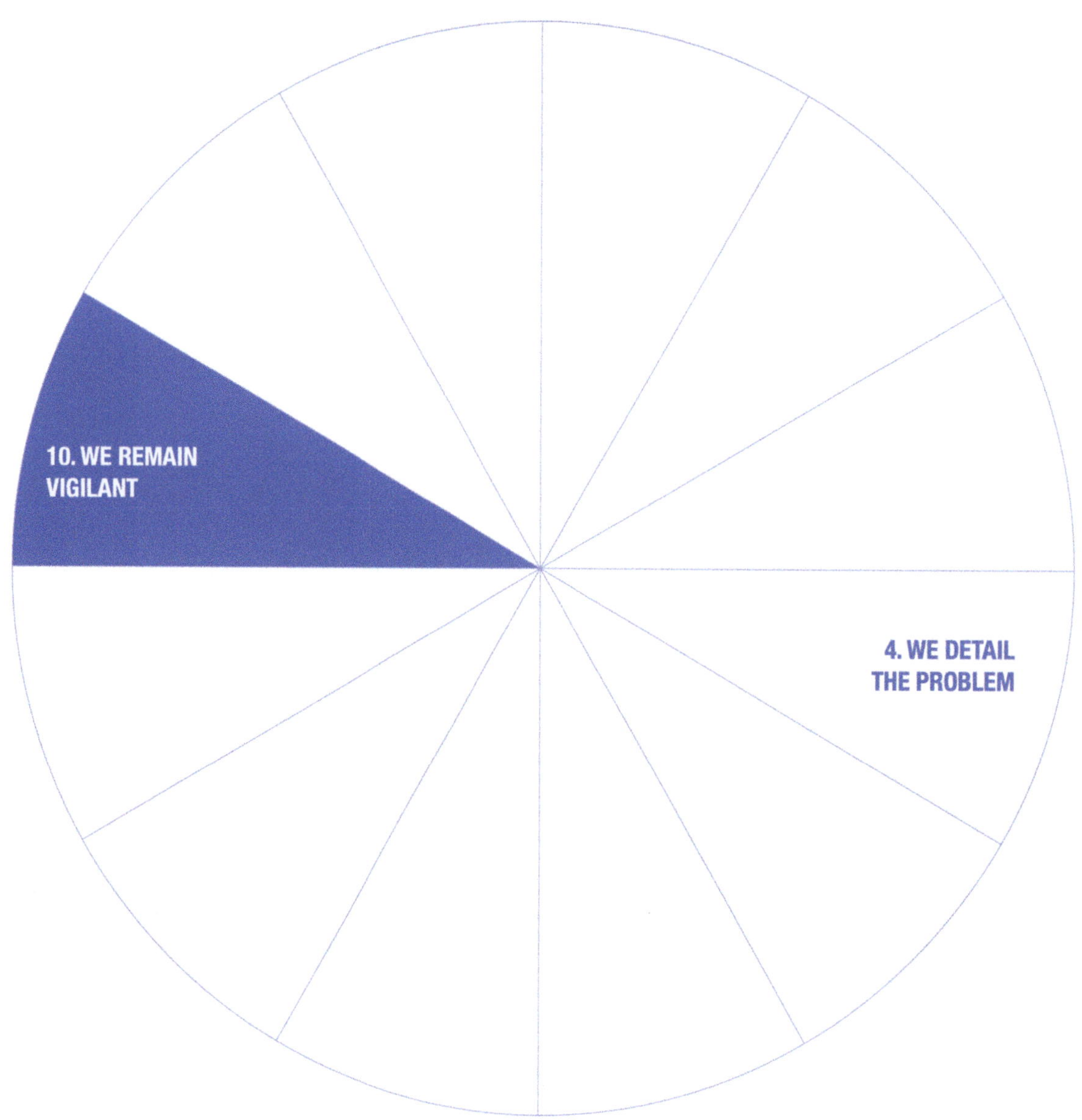

Relapse and recidivism can seem complex and insurmountable. Why are they so difficult?

How does "clearing out the wreckage of the past" ensure the United States' future?

COMPLETE ANY SECTION AS YOU ARE READY. BE CONCISE. REVIEW AS YOU PROGRESS.		
WHAT IS STEP 10? SAY IT AS YOU WRITE IT.	WHAT IS THE LEARNING OUTCOME FOR STEP 10?	WHAT ARE KEY WORDS FROM STEP 10?
STEP 10 DEPENDS ON STEP 4. DESCRIBE HOW.	WHAT ARE YOU LEARNING?	WHAT DOES DEMOCRACY REQUIRE? WHO DO YOU WANT TO BE? WHAT IS YOUR PLAN?

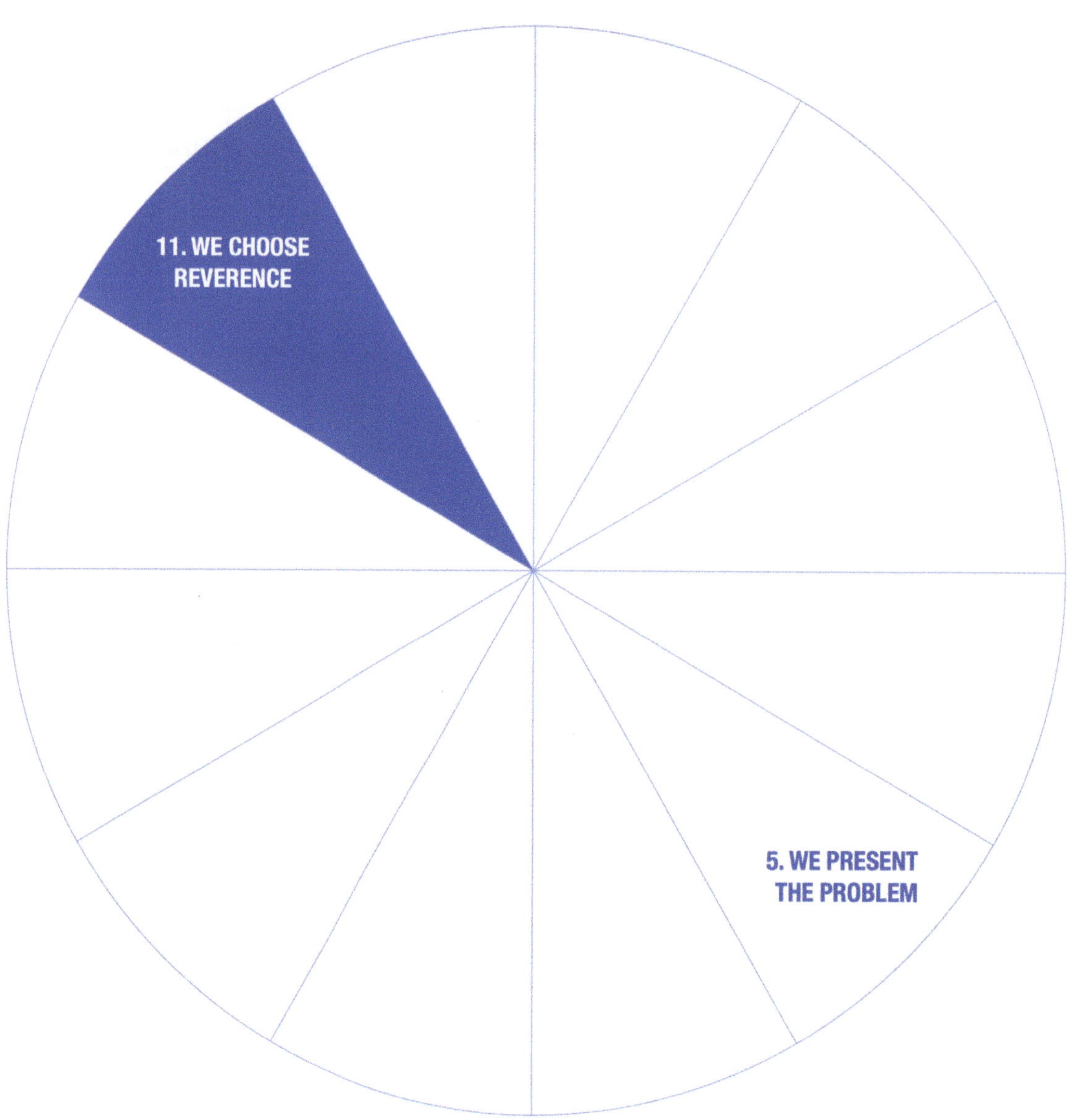

How does choosing to live equitably and justly invoke reverence?

What is *Ahimsa* and its role in the civil rights movement? What is *Asteya*?

COMPLETE ANY SECTION AS YOU ARE READY. BE CONCISE. REVIEW AS YOU PROGRESS.		
WHAT IS STEP 11? SAY IT AS YOU WRITE IT.	WHAT IS THE LEARNING OUTCOME FOR STEP 11?	WHAT ARE KEY WORDS FROM STEP 11?
STEP 11 DEPENDS ON STEP 5. DESCRIBE HOW.	WHAT ARE YOU LEARNING?	WHAT DOES DEMOCRACY REQUIRE? WHO DO YOU WANT TO BE? WHAT IS YOUR PLAN?

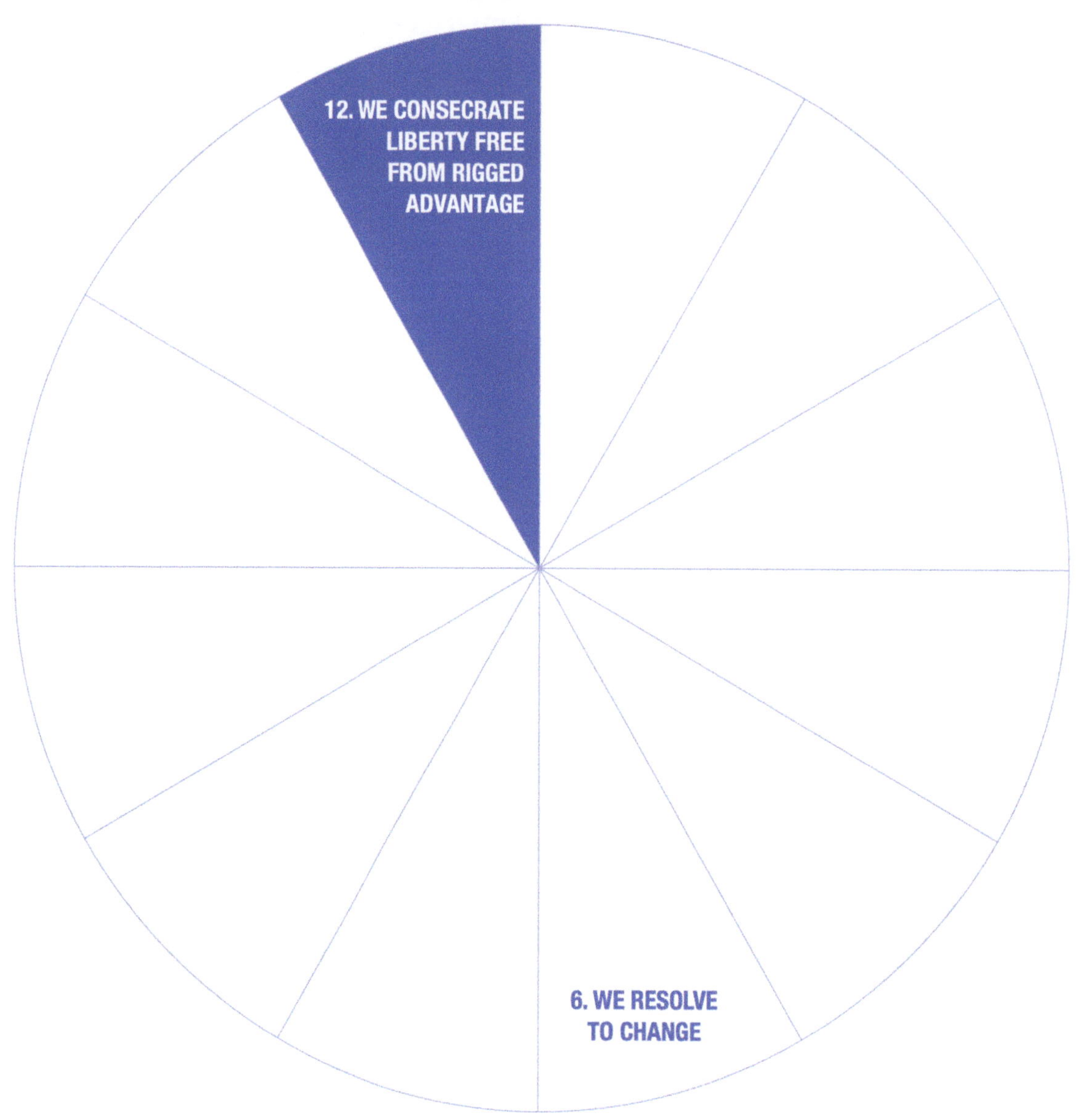

How does a “personal program of recovery” become a practice of principles in all affairs?

How can a self-imposed yoke also be a transcendent form of freedom?

COMPLETE ANY SECTION AS YOU ARE READY. BE CONCISE. REVIEW AS YOU PROGRESS.		
WHAT IS STEP 12? SAY IT AS YOU WRITE IT.	WHAT IS THE LEARNING OUTCOME FOR STEP 12?	WHAT ARE KEY WORDS FROM STEP 12?
STEP 12 DEPENDS ON STEP 6. DESCRIBE HOW.	WHAT ARE YOU LEARNING?	WHAT DOES DEMOCRACY REQUIRE? WHO DO YOU WANT TO BE? WHAT IS YOUR PLAN?

ADVANCED MASTERY EXERCISES

THE PRESUMPTION OF WHEREABOUTS AUTHORITY

Your authority over the location of another human being is limited.

Factors are not limited to the following:

- Supervisory relationship
- Past and current perceived social norms regarding, age, race, gender, socioeconomic status
- Role dynamics such as teacher–student, law enforcement–citizen

Consider the following:

- An essential part of slavery on plantations was the absolute right to authority over the whereabouts of enslaved people who were legally considered to be the property of the plantation owner.
- Violent retribution was the price to be paid if a slave was found *out of bounds*. Fugitive slave patrols were legally sanctioned. Whites in free northern states were legally required to cooperate.
- A minority (the owner and employees such as an overseer) ruled over the majority (the enslaved people who in most cases outnumbered the owners and employees).

Examples of Plantation Behavior and Ideology in Modern Life:

- Plantation slavery race habits[1] continued after the Civil War and persist in our present-day lives.

1 Glaude (2017).

- Presumption of whereabouts authority (PWA) over Black bodies was reimagined and sustained; see the following examples:

Legislation and judicial opinions such as *Plessy v. Ferguson*	Trumped up charges to produce incarcerated labor
Segregation of schools, transportation, and lunch counters	Sun-down towns
Miscegenation	Redlined neighborhoods
Overt domestic terrorism (e.g., Ku Klux Klan)	Tulsa, Wilmington, Thibodaux, Harperville
Minority rule	Limited economic participation
Poll taxes	Fugitive slave patrols masquerading as law enforcement
Covert domestic terrorism. Symbolic veneration of White Americans who had fought to own Black Americans: Confederate monuments	

- Since plantation slavery, the United States has struggled with whereabouts authority constantly resprouting in current events: police brutality; Charlottesville; insurrection with the Confederate flag in our Capitol overtaken by people shouting, "We own this, We own you"; Karens in Central Park, and "May I help you" personnel in retail.

GOAL: WHITE AMERICANS DISRUPT THE PRESUMPTION OF WHEREABOUTS AUTHORITY OVER BLACK AMERICANS.

It must be eliminated in all forms: voter intimidation, minority rule rigged through gerrymandering, and archaic governance, which thwarts the will of the people, or domestic terrorism designed to put Black Americans "in their place." Despite the legacies of slavery that resprout in current events to the contrary, democracy has no place for anyone to rule over another based on race.

HOW DOES RACE FACTOR REGARDING YOUR ENTITLEMENT TO EXERCISE AUTHORITY OVER THE WHEREABOUTS OF OTHERS?	
Learning Outcomes	**Tip**
• Recognize and analyze ideology leading to this presumption. • Identify and eliminate the presumption of authority over the whereabouts of Black Americans. • Recognize this behavior in current events and name it. • Identify and challenge this behavior in your networks.	The United States is a democracy ideally becoming a more perfect union where race will not predict the access to or the outcomes of democracy. It is not a country that some White Americans own and need to take back from another group. Citizenship works fervently toward the democratic goals that all Americans are created equal and entitled to certain inalienable rights. For Black Americans to increasingly take their seat at the table of democratic citizenship means that the United States is working, things are getting better, and the United States will be competitive and secure on the world stage for generations to come. Any White American who seeks to limit that seat at the table curtails justice and liberty and forecasts the demise of the American experiment with democracy. Those White Americans are in fact the thing they fear and project: a threat to the United States.

Exercise: The Presumption of Whereabouts Authority

If White Americans are not thinking they are perpetuating the plantation where they presume authority over the whereabouts of Black Americans, what could they be thinking? What is the motivation? What is happening?

___

___

___

___

What will you need to be able to identify and eliminate PWA in your community including the workplace?

___

___

___

___

List examples from current events where you believe PWA was problematic.

For future practice, note examples here regarding progress you see in yourself or others.

THE POWER DYNAMICS OF INTERRUPTION

Your entitlement to interrupt others is limited.

Factors are not limited to the following:

- Family-of-origin norms
- Current perceived social norms regarding, age, race, gender
- Socioeconomic status
- Role dynamics such as teacher–student, law enforcement–citizen

Consider the following:

- Historically, men have interrupted women with such entitlement that it was either hardly noticed or tolerated as acceptable.
- For a woman to interrupt a man proportionately may have earned her the double standard label "pushy" versus the label "assertive" for a man.

Example:

- A famous example is the 2020 televised vice presidential debate. Vice presidential candidate Kamala Harris countered Vice President Mike Pence's interruptions with, "Mr. Vice President, I'm speaking. I'm speaking."
- White children born into Jim Crow segregation were entitled to interrupt any elder who was a Black American. A Jim Crow White child was entitled to the sidewalk as well. Therefore, a Black American elder would expect an interruption of their passage on a sidewalk to ensure

the right of way for a Jim Crow White child. (For historical perspective, this occurred within President Obama's lifetime.)

GOAL

White Americans disrupt and end the race-based **entitlement to interrupt** (a legacy of slavery alive in the present) to support democracy where race must not predict democratic opportunities and outcomes.

HOW DOES RACE FACTOR REGARDING YOUR ENTITLEMENT TO INTERRUPT OTHERS?	
Learning Outcomes	**Tip**
• Reflect on your interrupting behaviors. • Identify any variance of entitlement to interrupt based on perceived race. Identify the origin of the behavior. • Modify the behavior to eliminate race as a factor when choosing to interrupt others.	If you are an employee, you may expect justifiable discipline when your interruption behavior compromises an organization's stated diversity, inclusion, and equity outcomes. What becomes an identifiable problem later may have begun with your entitlement to interrupt others based on race and gender. The following responses indicate limited insight and displaced responsibility: • I didn't intend to offend. • They shouldn't be so sensitive. • Why are they coming after me? • They're just playing the race card against me.

Exercise: The Power Dynamics of Interruption

How do people learn about interruption in communication?

How does interrupting someone reflect self-perceived status?

What are examples from current situations where you believe interrupting others was problematic?

For future practice, note examples here regarding progress you see in yourself or others.

FUNDAMENTAL CHANGE PRINCIPLE: FIRST THINGS FIRST

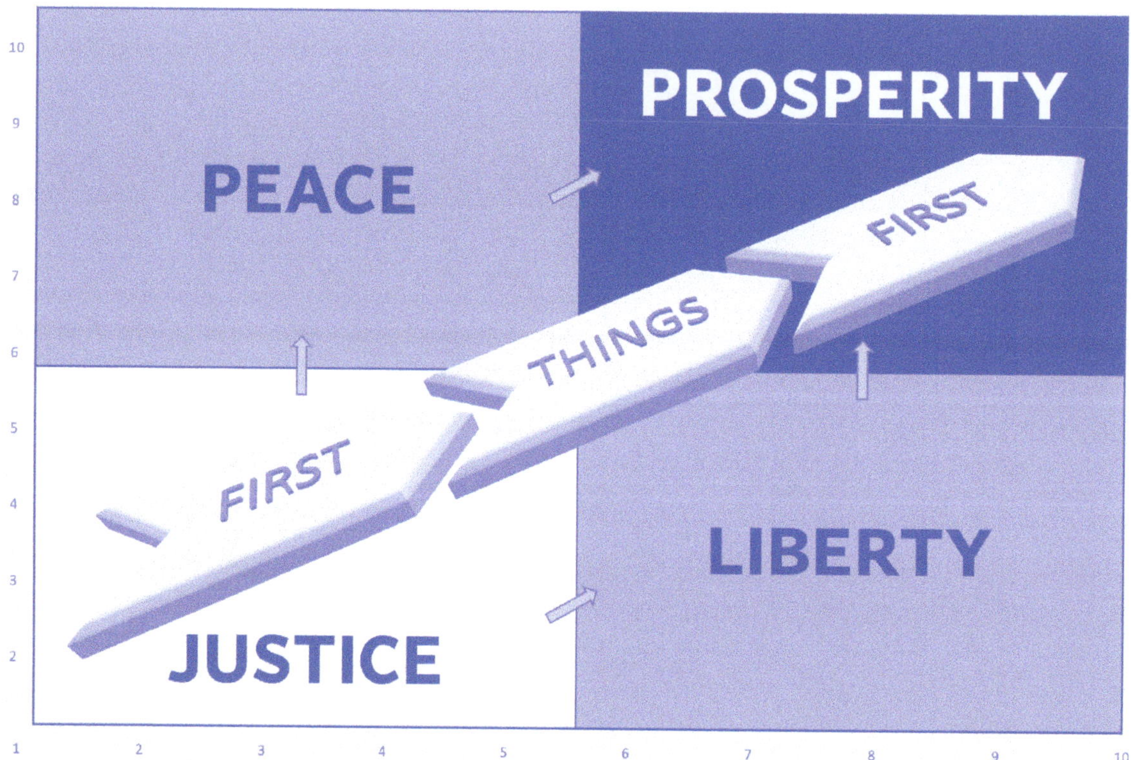

Old Habits

Old habits die hard. This is a fundamental principle of change. Even when our way of life may be destructive and deadly, we cling. It is all we know. Ask a recovering alcoholic about it if you want a fresh and raw perspective on what change is all about. To survive, a recovering alcoholic ventures into a new land, with no money, no language, no history, no self to rely on. How overwhelming!

Pithy Sayings: Lifesavers

The recovery community begins to teach a newcomer not only with the 12 steps but also with pithy sayings. At first, their simplicity is nearly mockable until they become all you can hold onto to make it 1 more day. "First things first" is such a lifesaver. In the throes of intense relapse-prone moments where life may be bearing down hard, just focusing on the next right thing is all you can do.

New Territory

When it comes to dismantling rigged advantage, some of you will be venturing into new territory. Your reflexes may howl for diversion. Rationalization, projection, displacement, denial, insult, and more will overwhelm you. Instead of venturing into this new land called democracy, you may wail to "get your country back." This equivalent of getting drunk again does not bode well for you. Crucially, the rest of us cannot tolerate your addiction to rigged advantage anymore. We can no longer afford to sit in your living room while you set the kitchen on fire.

Can't Skip Straight to Prosperity

When you feel the heat of democracy and start craving rigged advantage, you must practice first things first. You must ask yourself, "What is the next right thing to do to make it through a triggered moment?" Rigged advantage has historically enabled too many White Americans to pass justice and peace and go straight to liberty to sustain prosperity for an elite few. It may be what you are feeling when you sing "Proud to be an American, where at least I know I'm free," but that is out of order. It is dysfunctional. You are not entitled to it.

Sustainable Democracy

The sustainable order of democracy is justice, then peace, then liberty, then prosperity. First things first. It may seem normal that nothing matters but prosperity. If you are prosperous and a generational inheritance entitles you to such a future, we celebrate you. But, in a democracy that is sustainable, you must get to such a future justly, peaceably, and in liberty.

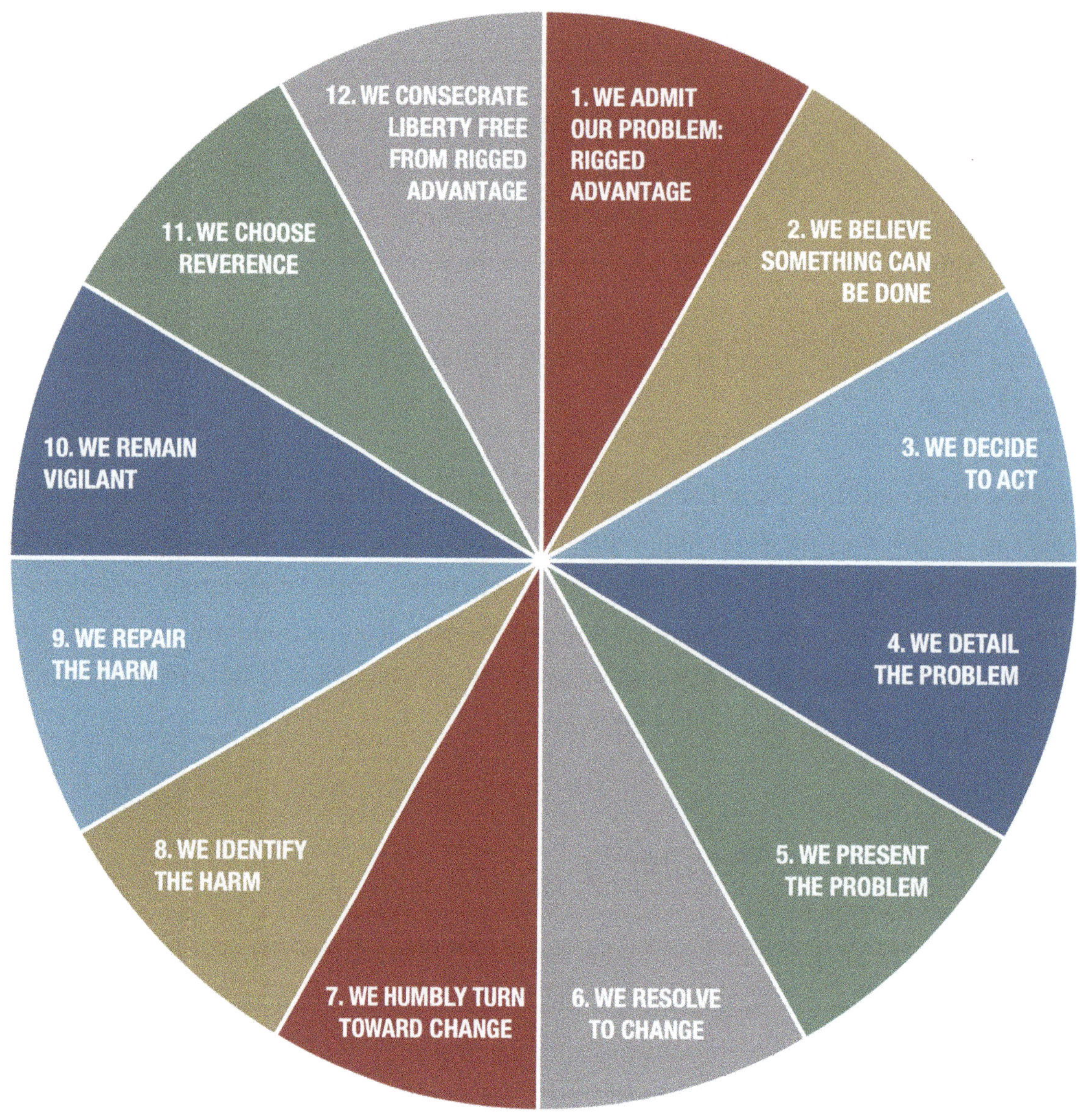

Exercise: First Things First

How is justice then liberty for some and not others normalized?

____

____

____

____

Why are old habits (instead of what we recently learned) relied on when we are stressed?

What can be problematic about a nation that is prosperous but the middle class is shrinking?

White entitlement to prosperity without a foundation of justice for all threatens U.S. security and global competitiveness. Why? How?

MATURITY SEEKING MASTERY: LOVING KINDNESS MEDITATION

The loving kindness meditation is an ancient practice of compassion.* Customize this for yourself. For example, you could begin the meditation with "May I be filled with gratitude for my wonderful life" and end the meditation with "May I wish these things for all beings in all places at all times."

*This exercise is inspired by Kornfield, J. (2008). *Guided meditation: Six essential practices to cultivate love, awareness, and wisdom* [Album]. Sounds True.

THIS IS A MASTERY TOOL YOU USE TO MANAGE YOURSELF FOR YOUR SAKE.

Insert an image of the person(s) who are the subject of your meditation. Begin the practice with yourself.

Graduate to even the most dangerous person or groups. Spend as much time at each level as like. Return to any level whenever you like.

	INSERT DESIRED IMAGE	RECITE MEDITATION	
Self	IMG 4.3	May I be filled with loving kindness. May I be well in body and mind. May I be safe from inner and outer dangers. May I be truly happy and free.	**Beginner Novice**
Loved One		May you be filled with loving kindness. May you be well in body and mind. May you be safe from inner and outer dangers. May you be truly happy and free.	**Beginner Developing**
Acquaintance		May you be filled with loving kindness. May you be well in body and mind. May you be safe from inner and outer dangers. May you be truly happy and free.	**Beginner Emergent Mastery**
Stranger		May you be filled with loving kindness. May you be well in body and mind. May you be safe from inner and outer dangers. May you be truly happy and free.	**Intermediate Moderate Mastery**
Person of Concern		May you be filled with loving kindness. May you be well in body and mind. May you be safe from inner and outer dangers. May you be truly happy and free.	**Advanced Significant Mastery**
Person of Threat		May you be filled with loving kindness. May you be well in body and mind. May you be safe from inner and outer dangers. May you be truly happy and free.	**Advanced Master**
Person of Danger		May you be filled with loving kindness. May you be well in body and mind. May you be safe from inner and outer dangers. May you be truly happy and free.	**Advanced Master State of Grace**

Exercise: Loving Kindness

We can get stuck in our judgmental prosecution of ourselves and others. How can this meditation relieve our resentment habits? Can this practice help us if resentments are planted in us by and for others?

In some ways, loving those who love us is even easier than loving ourselves. Loving those who do not love us is more difficult. Loving your enemies is a known principle of liberation and transcendence, but its practice is extremely rare. Why is it difficult to intend good for *all* beings in *all* places and *all* times?

Atonement sounds very religious, but "at - one - ment" makes it simple. For our purposes, atonement means doing what is necessary for accord. The United States must be in one accord (*E pluribus unum* is the U.S. motto) to experience atonement (not a house divided). Rigged advantage = discord. Dismantling rigged advantage is the repair pathway to accord. Can you make way for repair even if you cannot possibly imagine what repair could be? *(Pro tip: It would require a greater vision than resentment permits.)*

Truth Repentance Reconciliation Atonement Renewal Redemption

This sequence (a summary of 12SWA) will be impossible without the mastery of loving kindness toward self and others.

This mastery is fundamental to realizing the steps. But how do you do something you have not mastered?

Alcoholics know something about this. They know that as they are getting sober, they must not drink but they do not yet have what it takes. They take it 1 day at a time. They fake it until they make it. They let go and let God. They practice first things first. They just do the next right thing. They clear out the wreckage of their past. They work their steps. They get rid of stinking thinking. They pray for knowledge of God's will and for the power to carry that out. They practice the principles of getting sober in all their affairs. They practice rigorous honesty. With enormous gratitude for a new life that had been unimaginable, they help other alcoholics experience a second chance that they know is miraculous because they have experienced it firsthand. They become so clearly convinced of their need for change that they are willing to go to any lengths.

The United States of America—a sober USA no longer drunk in a death spiral of rigged advantage—is worth whatever mastery is necessary. The ideals that potentiate our future are hard-won ancestral blessings we now squander while drunk, decadent, and decayed in the immorality of inequality's excess and the legacies of slavery unabated.

White America must stop, turn, make things right, and make way for all so our best days are ahead of us.

Loving kindness may sound trite, but make no mistake, the future of a great democracy depends on it.

RACIAL WEALTH INEQUALITY

The United States has not recovered from plantation slavery.

Insufficient Black American "progress," from being property to having property, compromises the integrity and future of the United States.

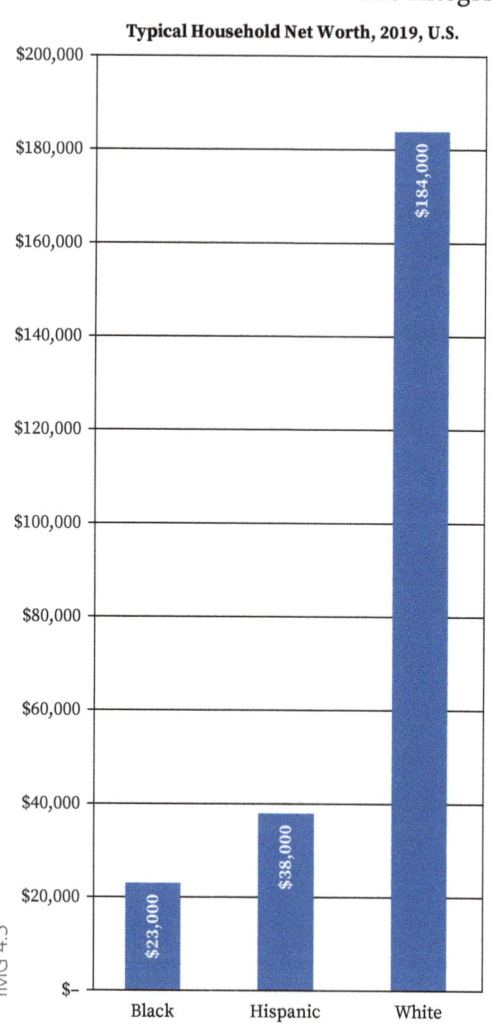

Has wealth inequality in America changed over time? Here are key statistics.

IMG 4.5

"Income disparities are as big as in the pre-civil rights era.

In 1950, the income of the median white household was about twice as high as the income of the median black household.

In 2016, black household income is still only half of the income of white households.

The racial wealth gap is even wider and remains as large as it was in the 1950s & 1960s.

The median black household persistently has less than 15% of the wealth of the median white household.

Over seven decades, next to no progress has been made in closing the black-white income gap.

The racial wealth gap is equally persistent and a stark fact of postwar American history.

The typical black household remains poorer than 80% of white households."

The financial crisis hit black households particularly hard and has undone the little progress that had been made in reducing the racial wealth gap during the 2000s.[1]

FEDERAL RESERVE BANK OF MINNEAPOLIS

1 Kuhn, M., Schularick, M., & Steins, U. I. (2020). Income and wealth inequality in America, 1949–2016. *Journal of Political Economy, 128*(9).

Exercise: Idealized Versus Realized America

How can minority rule sustain rigged advantage well into the future despite demographic inevitabilities?

The socioeconomic progress we have realized is overrated by many White Americans. The study "Misperception of Racial Economic Equality," by Kraus et al. showed that the actual extreme of racial household wealth inequality is vastly *underestimated*.[2]

- Why do you believe this is the case? Would people vote for different policies if they knew the facts?
- Who benefits from the presumption of progress when, according to the Federal Reserve Bank of Minneapolis, "no progress has been made in reducing income and wealth inequalities between black and white households over the past 70 years"?

People who work for improving U.S. socioeconomic indicators are often ostracized as "socialists."

- How can it be true that some White Americans who ostracize economic justice work would themselves benefit from economic justice but, instead, they vote against their own interests?
- Who benefits from the mentality "America—love it or leave it"?

2 Kraus, M. W., Rucker, J. M., & Richeson, J. A. (2017). Americans misperceive racial economic equality. Proceedings of the National Academy of Sciences, 114(39), 10324–10331. https://doi.org/10.1073/pnas.1707719114

TEST YOUR KNOWLEDGE REGARDING SOCIOECONOMIC DISPARITIES IN THE UNITED STATES

CIRCLE TRUE OR FALSE

T	F	1. Over 7 decades, next to no progress has been made in closing the Black-White income gap.
T	F	2. Income disparities between Blacks and Whites are as big as the pre-civil rights era.
T	F	3. The median Black household persistently has less than 15% of the wealth of the median White household.
T	F	4. The financial crisis hit Black households particularly hard. It has undone the little progress that had been made in reducing the racial wealth gap during the 2000s.
T	F	5. In 2016, Black household income is still only half of the income of White households.
T	F	6. The typical Black household remains poorer than 80% of White households.
T	F	7. Most Americans vastly underestimate the racial wealth gap. "a profound misperception of and misplaced optimism regarding contemporary societal racial economic equality—a misperception that is likely to have important consequences for public policy."

ANSWER KEY 1. T 2. T 3. T 4. T 5. T 6. T 7. T **SEE WORKBOOK PAGE** 76

TRUE AT THE SAME TIME

- **TRUE: Median White American households have eight times the wealth of Black American households.**
- **TRUE: More White Americans than Black Americans receive "welfare benefits."**

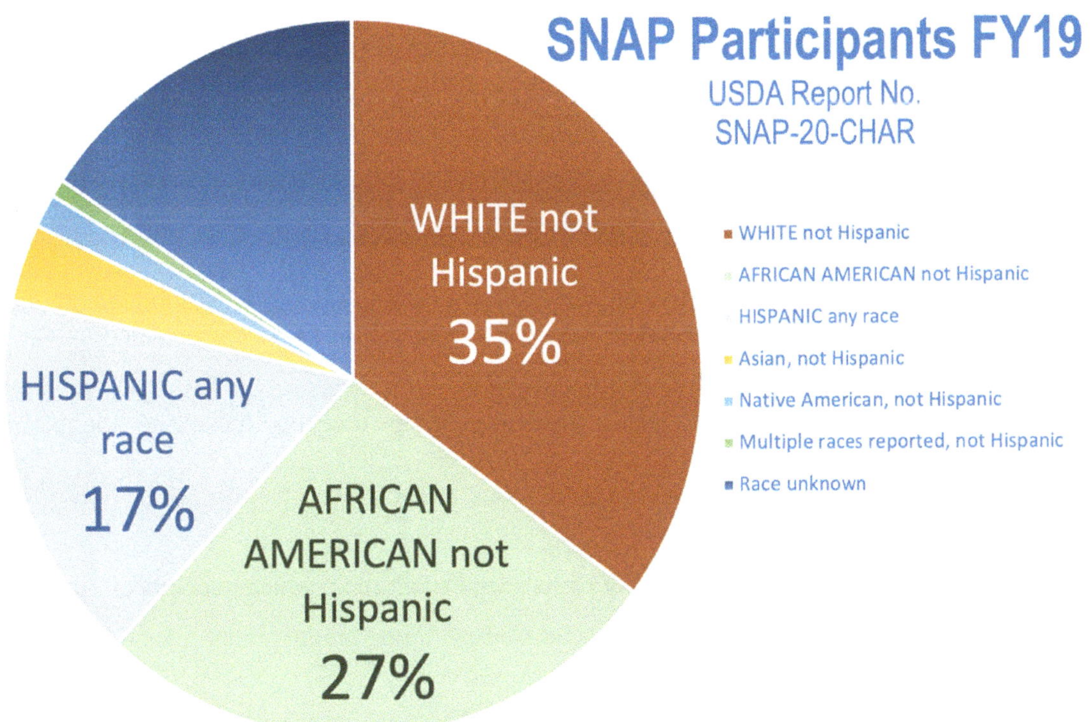

Inequality increasingly shifts wealth to an elite few power Whites. Exploited Whites (and others) are correct that they are losing something that they had.

Describe the implications for policy when so many White people are struggling to make ends meet while hearing that rigged advantage disproportionately benefits White Americans.

IDEOLOGICAL RIGIDITY: IMPERMEABILITY

Ideological rigidity in the United States has been calcified by at least two major developments:

- the ideological homogenization of **gerrymandered districts** whose elected officials are rewarded for resisting legislative compromise and
- the **clustering of information** delivery systems (for profit) into homogenous echo chambers where minimal permeability exists.

DISCUSSION: ARE FREEDOM AND JUSTICE A ZERO-SUM GAME?

Freedom and justice are ideals in progress. Freedom and justice may appear to compete in what can be perceived to be a zero-sum game. (Your freedom compromises my justice. My justice diminishes your freedom.)

- Traditionally, Democrats venerate justice for all even when that may present to Republicans as curtailing freedoms.
- Traditionally, Republicans venerate freedom even when that may present to Democrats as compromising justice.

The conditioning of ideological impermeability limits social adaptation, which depends on cooperation.

- Like an addiction that overtakes rational survival, ideological impermeability cuts its nose off to spite its face.
- Immediate triggers outweigh longer term value.
- Situational permeability for adaptive purposes becomes tests of ideological purity.
- Variance or deviance is subject to excommunication (or what is increasingly known as cancel culture).
- Excommunication sustains purity but diminishes traits for adaptation, cooperation, and permeability across ideology—even situationally such as during times of crises or rare opportunity.

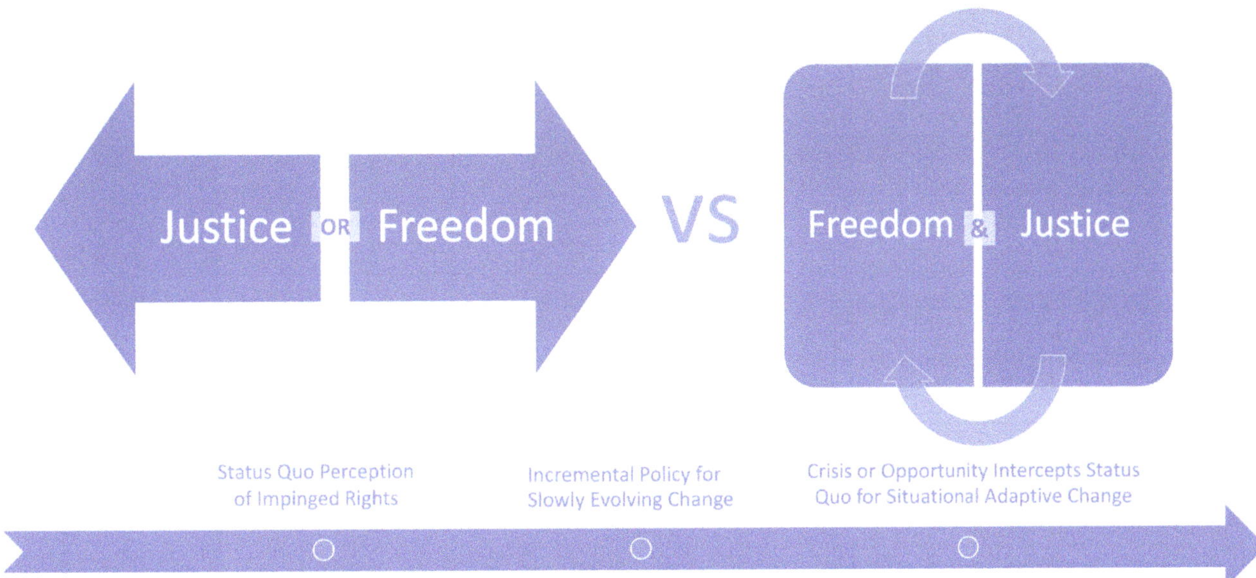

Exercise: Idealized Versus Realized America

How does a gerrymandered district representative choose voters versus voters choosing that representative?

____

____

____

____

What are two developments that have calcified ideological rigidity?

____

____

____

____

What is "cancel culture," and how does it work?

What do addiction and ideological rigidity have in common?

3D POWER CONTROLS NARRATIVE: DOMINANCE, DEFENSE, DELIVERANCE

Biblical scripture was used to justify the Atlantic Slave Trade in the Americas.

The following parses a review of this narrative operating system.
The biblical justification
(*reasoning*)
for slavery to build and sustain rigged advantage was a scriptural
(*sacred words*)
excerpt
(*words among words*)
from a testament
(*worded agreement/contract*)
to sanction
(*storied enactment of state authority*)
the practice
(*policy—written and inferred will of people in power*)
of shackling some human beings for commerce
(*trade regulated by law writings*)
by other human beings who colluded that
(*coherence with the accepted cultural narrative*)
sustaining their rigged advantage was a divine
entitlement, not unlike divine right of kings
(*consistent with the origin God story that ordered their lives*).

The human beings who controlled this narrative enslaved millions of other human beings, exploited their labor, and produced economic prosperity to catapult the United States into existence and then emerge as a dominant world power.

Controlling the Narrative Is Alive and Well

Virginia's prohibition of critical race theory today extends a lineage of U.S. antiliteracy laws prohibiting the education of enslaved persons. Then, literacy directly threatened slavery. Today, it threatens slavery continuously reimagined as rigged advantage. The contradiction persists: an elite few power Whites oppressing the liberty of others using dominance, defense, and the promise of deliverance for the exploited White Americans who do their bidding.

SAMPLE OF A DAILY PROGRAM OF PRACTICE

The 12th step of AA says, "Having had a spiritual awakening as the result of these steps, we tried to carry this message to alcoholics, and to practice these principles in all our affairs." For alcoholics, recovery is not an isolated management system to control remission of alcoholism; rather, the principles (the same principles that inform #12SWA) become a way of life applied to every circumstance, even when it may seem unrelated to alcoholism. For the author, more than 3 decades of practicing the 12-step program of recovery means that applying the principles to the issue of rigged advantage in the United States is a natural extension—just another day of applying recovery principles "in all our affairs."

The following set of questions on the next page comprise a sample of a daily program or practice.

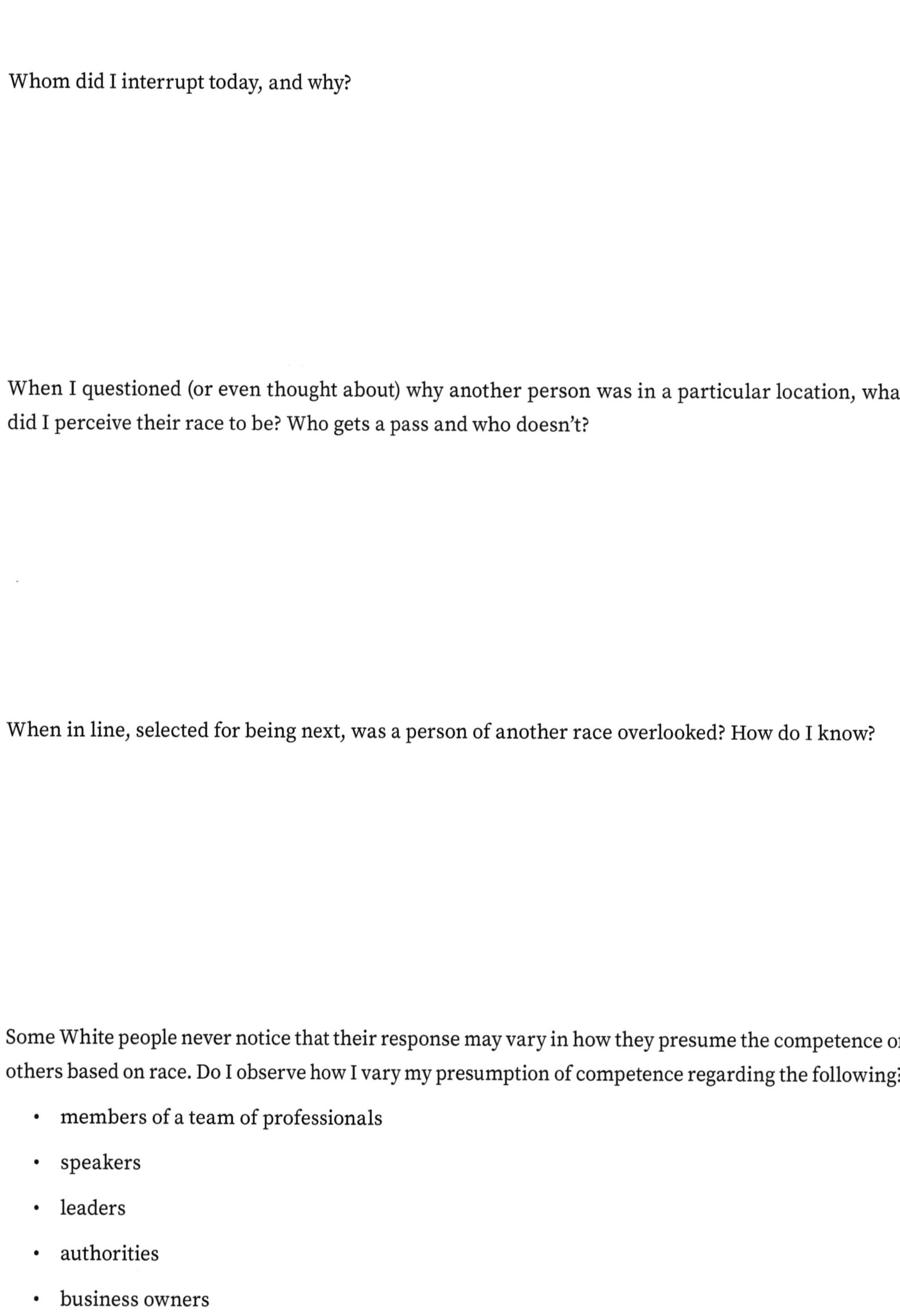

Whom did I interrupt today, and why?

When I questioned (or even thought about) why another person was in a particular location, what did I perceive their race to be? Who gets a pass and who doesn't?

When in line, selected for being next, was a person of another race overlooked? How do I know?

Some White people never notice that their response may vary in how they presume the competence of others based on race. Do I observe how I vary my presumption of competence regarding the following?

- members of a team of professionals
- speakers
- leaders
- authorities
- business owners

- contract bidders
- students
- applicants
- interviewees
- delivery personnel
- doctors
- college presidents
- financial advisors
- investors
- philanthropists
- therapists
- news reporters
- neighbors
- police officers
- online support personnel

Do I believe that race is no longer an opportunity factor when variables such as educational attainment and income are controlled? Is my conclusion based on reliable research?

Are some English language accents presumed to represent more capable or cultured individuals than others? What role does race/ethnicity/country of origin play in your presumption?

Does the degree to which I tolerate socially awkward or inappropriate behavior vary based on race? How do I know?

The research shows disproportionate benefit for White people based on several indicators:
Do I set my intention daily to be conscious of (or account for) the privilege afforded to me?
In what ways do I specifically get a pass? In what ways do I receive advantage?
If I believe I don't benefit, how do I know? Do I want to find out?

Does disproportionate sentencing within our justice system correlate with disproportionate criminality among Black and Brown people? Is my conclusion based on reliable research?

White people have historically presumed the right to control or inform the whereabouts of people of color. This perceived entitlement is about controlling the whereabouts of enslaved people and sharecroppers: "Where are you supposed to be?"

- When approaching others to help, am I masking an entitled intention to control others in a given situation?
- Am I entitled to that information? Did their perceived race matter? How do I know for sure?

When presuming competence, do some English language errors get more of a pass from me than others? Are those mistakes stereotypically attributed to a particular race or race/region or race/class combination? How do I know if I do this or not?

Do I consistently respond to those seeking my attention without racial bias impacting my response?
Do I notice or pay attention to incoming information or requests without bias?
How do I know? Have I ever questioned this to be sure?

Do I instantly notice the racial makeup of a room? If I don't, how do I know if that is a privilege others aren't afforded?

How often in the last week was I the only White person in the room?

How often last week did someone refer to me being White without it being relevant information? Do I know how often this happens to my friends, family members, or colleagues who are perceived as non-White?

Am I aware of any within-race biases? Do I collude with those biases? How do I know?

Do I know or have I known a person who self-identifies with a non-White race but is perceived as White? What have I learned from their experiences?

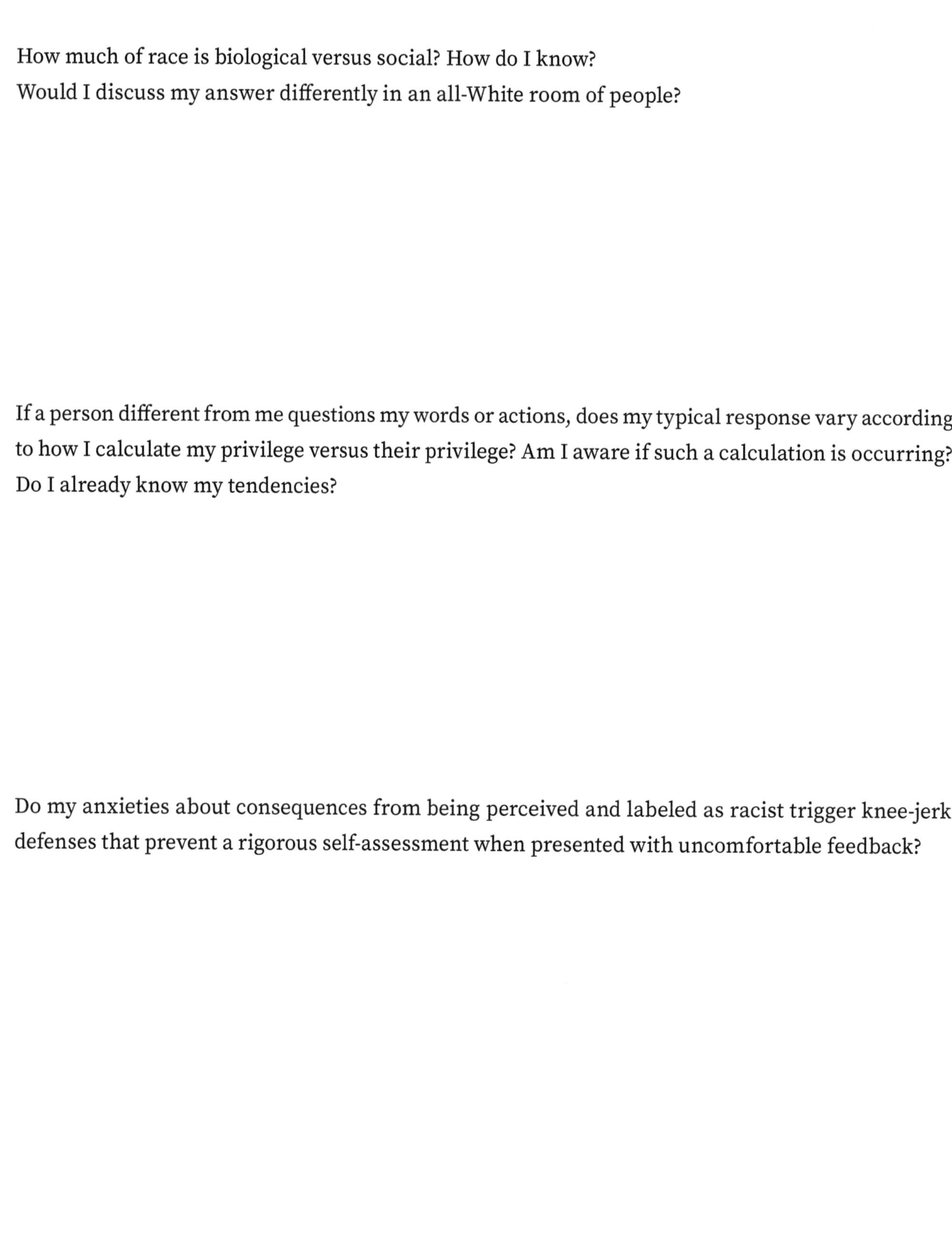

How much of race is biological versus social? How do I know?
Would I discuss my answer differently in an all-White room of people?

If a person different from me questions my words or actions, does my typical response vary according to how I calculate my privilege versus their privilege? Am I aware if such a calculation is occurring? Do I already know my tendencies?

Do my anxieties about consequences from being perceived and labeled as racist trigger knee-jerk defenses that prevent a rigorous self-assessment when presented with uncomfortable feedback?

In the context of these anxieties and the triggered defensiveness that results, do I require others to appease my concerns without addressing theirs? For example, if I said or did something perceived as racist and got called on it, do I demand a pass because I do not believe I *intended* to be racist or be perceived as racist?

Am I capable of addressing the actual racist result of my words or actions even if I don't believe I intended it? On a 10-point scale measuring a continuum from rigidity to flexibility, how flexible is my response-ability in addressing the impact of my words or actions when I did not intend that result?

Do I understand that it is common among people of color to calculate how their words and actions will disturb White people? Do I understand that this dynamic of the oppressed appeasing oppressors has a long legacy in the United States common from slavery plantations?

Image Credits

IMG 4.3: Copyright © 2019 Depositphotos/iconscart.

IMG 4.5: Ana Hernandez Kent and Lowell Ricketts, "Typical Household Net Worth, 2019, U.S.," https://www.stlouisfed.org/open-vault/2020/december/has-wealth-inequality-changed-over-time-key-statistics. Copyright © 2020 by Federal Reserve Bank of St. Louis.

APPENDIX: THE FOURTH STEP—CONTEXTUALIZING FAMILY HISTORY, CHRISTINE SLEETER, PhD

Situate your life in the context of the America journey.

What Is Contextualizing Family History?

Traditional genealogy is concerned with family trees.
Contextualizing family history (CFH) provides a tool to support accounting for historical contexts. **Christine Sleeter, PhD,** has published fiction and nonfiction enriching traditional approaches to genealogy with a wider analysis of social power relationships and culture.

Why Is It Important?

- In traditional recovery programs, step 4, inventory/accounting, clarifies explicitly what we need to work on to "clear out the wreckage of past."
- Step 4 enables us to anticipate the land mines that may derail our recovery. Also, CFH provides information we will need in step 8 (identify the harm).
- Knowing our family tree in the context of their lives provides us with a richer understanding of our own beginnings. We also get a deeper understanding of the baggage accumulated along the way of remarkable journeys. In short, we come to know not only *who* but *how* and *why it matters today.*

How Do I Do It?

- Use the framework on the following pages. (Many people know little about traditional genealogy and nothing about how to contextualize it. If you do not need a framework, do not let this get in your way.)
- Use the CFH tables that follow. Determine in what ways your ancestors have colluded with, perpetuated, or been complicit in racism specifically, as well as in sexism, classism, and religious oppression.
- Identify if/how they benefited.

- At the end of your list, *include yourself* as though you are an ancestor to the next generation. *Take your own inventory.* How have/do your own ideologies and actions collude with *and* perpetuate rigged advantage?

When Do I Do It?

- The work of each step is a straightforward two-page exercise, except the fourth step. Here, you are also presented with the CFH assessment, a "deeper dive" in your fourth step work.
- **Do not let this derail you from completing steps 5–12.** If you prefer to wait, you could complete just the two-page exercise for step 4, continue completing the two-page exercise for steps 5–12, and then return to CFH as a more thorough exploration.
    - Recommendation: If you choose this option, review what the CFH entails and briefly note what you may already know, then
    - return to the CFH to more fully reveal the goldmine, which is the story of how you came to be, and situate your life in the context of the America journey to

Unshackle the past,
strengthen U.S. security and global competitiveness, and
make way for all so that our best days are ahead of us.

Contextualized Genealogical Research Tools

Christine Sleeter, PhD

Resources for Documentation

Family documents
Oral history interviews
Census records (including "Slave Schedules")
Religious records
Military records
Digitized newspapers such as *Chronicling America* (crowdsourced) and Directory of Historical Newspapers on the internet
Subscription services such as Ancestry.com, newspaper archive
Primary accounts written at the time
Historically researched accounts
Artifacts

Contextualizing Questions

Historical Context
What were global, national, and local events that impacted choices and opportunities?
When did a given event occur (date or date range or era)?
What laws had an impact on choices and opportunities?

Social Context
Who else was around?
Who was not there who could have or should have been?
What values, norms, and traditions were prevalent?
What economic, political, and/or cultural systems, conditions, or specific circumstances had impact?

Hidden Four "P" Factors (RE: Immigration)
Push factors: What drives people to emigrate from their country of origin?
Pull factors: What are desirable and favorable conditions that motivate change?
Punishing factors: What are the negative experiences that punish or marginalize people upon arrival?
Privileging factors: What are positive incentives or resources that privilege people upon arrival?

Additional Readings/Resources

Personal Stories From Genealogical Research in the Journal Genealogy
Edited By Christine Sleeter (https://www.mdpi.com/si/24136)

Mica Pollock: Flipping Our Scripts About Undocumented Immigration
Chantae Still: What It Means for Her Grandmother to "Walk Tall"
Avril Bell: Reverberating Historical Privilege

Personal Stories From Genealogical Research at the Christinesleeter.Org Blog
Traci Wilson-Kleekamp: Esoteric Clues (www.christinesleeter.org/esoteric-clues)
Brenda Johnson: Four Generations of One Family's Perspectives on Racism (www.christinesleeter.org/perspectives-on-racism)

Personal Stories From the PBS Series, Finding Your Roots
With Henry Louis Gates, Jr., Alphonse Fletcher University Professor and Director of the Hutchins Center for African & African American Research at Harvard University (https://www.pbs.org/weta/finding-your-roots/)

Contextualizing Family History

Christine Sleeter, PhD

Family History Typically Consists of Identifying Who, What, When, and Where.
Contextualizing Family History Enriches Our Understanding With a Wider Analysis of Social Power Relationships and Culture.

DIRECTIONS:	**USE THIS TOOL TO ENRICH WHO, WHAT, WHEN, AND WHERE. IDENTIFY HOW CONTEXT SHAPED YOUR ANCESTORS' WORLDS.** **HOW DID THEIR OPPORTUNITIES AND CHOICES LEAD TO YOU? EACH ANCESTOR MAY REQUIRE MULTIPLE ROWS.**					
WHO ANCESTOR	**WHAT** EVENT or MILESTONE	**WHEN** DATE, DATE RANGE, OR ERA	**WHERE** COMMUNITY, TOWN/CITY, OR COUNTRY	**SOCIO CULTURAL** PROPERTY, EDUCATION, LANGUAGE, NORMS, BELIEFS, HEALTH, ACCESS TO WEALTH TOOLS, MEMBERSHIPS/ AFFILIATIONS	**RELEVANT HISTORY** LAWS, POLITICS, POLICIES, CONFLICTS, ADVANCES, SLAVERY, IMMIGRATION, VOTING RIGHTS, COLONIZATION, INCARCERATION	**COMPARE/CONTRAST** OTHER GROUPS, POWER RELATIONSHIPS, STATUS, ADVANTAGE, OPPORTUNITY, RESISTANCE/ BREECHING OF NORMS

WHO ANCESTOR	**WHAT** EVENT or MILESTONE	**WHEN** DATE, DATE RANGE, OR ERA	**WHERE** COMMUNITY, TOWN/CITY, OR COUNTRY	**SOCIO CULTURAL** PROPERTY, EDUCATION, LANGUAGE, NORMS, BELIEFS, HEALTH, ACCESS TO WEALTH TOOLS, MEMBERSHIPS/ AFFILIATIONS	**RELEVANT HISTORY** LAWS, POLITICS, POLICIES, CONFLICTS, ADVANCES, SLAVERY, IMMIGRATION, VOTING RIGHTS, COLONIZATION, INCARCERATION	**COMPARE/CONTRAST** OTHER GROUPS, POWER RELATIONSHIPS, STATUS, ADVANTAGE, OPPORTUNITY, RESISTANCE/ BREECHING OF NORMS

WHO ANCESTOR	**WHAT** EVENT or MILESTONE	**WHEN** DATE, DATE RANGE, OR ERA	**WHERE** COMMUNITY, TOWN/CITY, OR COUNTRY	**SOCIO CULTURAL** PROPERTY, EDUCATION, LANGUAGE, NORMS, BELIEFS, HEALTH, ACCESS TO WEALTH TOOLS, MEMBERSHIPS/ AFFILIATIONS	**RELEVANT HISTORY** LAWS, POLITICS, POLICIES, CONFLICTS, ADVANCES, SLAVERY, IMMIGRATION, VOTING RIGHTS, COLONIZATION, INCARCERATION	**COMPARE/CONTRAST** OTHER GROUPS, POWER RELATIONSHIPS, STATUS, ADVANTAGE, OPPORTUNITY, RESISTANCE/ BREECHING OF NORMS

WHO ANCESTOR	**WHAT** EVENT or MILESTONE	**WHEN** DATE, DATE RANGE, OR ERA	**WHERE** COMMUNITY, TOWN/CITY, OR COUNTRY	**SOCIO CULTURAL** PROPERTY, EDUCATION, LANGUAGE, NORMS, BELIEFS, HEALTH, ACCESS TO WEALTH TOOLS, MEMBERSHIPS/ AFFILIATIONS	**RELEVANT HISTORY** LAWS, POLITICS, POLICIES, CONFLICTS, ADVANCES, SLAVERY, IMMIGRATION, VOTING RIGHTS, COLONIZATION, INCARCERATION	**COMPARE/CONTRAST** OTHER GROUPS, POWER RELATIONSHIPS, STATUS, ADVANTAGE, OPPORTUNITY, RESISTANCE/ BREECHING OF NORMS

WHO ANCESTOR	**WHAT** EVENT or MILESTONE	**WHEN** DATE, DATE RANGE, OR ERA	**WHERE** COMMUNITY, TOWN/CITY, OR COUNTRY	**SOCIO CULTURAL** PROPERTY, EDUCATION, LANGUAGE, NORMS, BELIEFS, HEALTH, ACCESS TO WEALTH TOOLS, MEMBERSHIPS/ AFFILIATIONS	**RELEVANT HISTORY** LAWS, POLITICS, POLICIES, CONFLICTS, ADVANCES, SLAVERY, IMMIGRATION, VOTING RIGHTS, COLONIZATION, INCARCERATION	**COMPARE/CONTRAST** OTHER GROUPS, POWER RELATIONSHIPS, STATUS, ADVANTAGE, OPPORTUNITY, RESISTANCE/ BREECHING OF NORMS

WHO ANCESTOR	**WHAT** EVENT or MILESTONE	**WHEN** DATE, DATE RANGE, OR ERA	**WHERE** COMMUNITY, TOWN/CITY, OR COUNTRY	**SOCIO CULTURAL** PROPERTY, EDUCATION, LANGUAGE, NORMS, BELIEFS, HEALTH, ACCESS TO WEALTH TOOLS, MEMBERSHIPS/ AFFILIATIONS	**RELEVANT HISTORY** LAWS, POLITICS, POLICIES, CONFLICTS, ADVANCES, SLAVERY, IMMIGRATION, VOTING RIGHTS, COLONIZATION, INCARCERATION	**COMPARE/CONTRAST** OTHER GROUPS, POWER RELATIONSHIPS, STATUS, ADVANTAGE, OPPORTUNITY, RESISTANCE/ BREECHING OF NORMS

INSERT ANCESTOR NAME HERE:	
CATEGORIZE YOUR FINDINGS ABOUT EACH ANCESTOR. (COPY AND USE THIS TABLE MULTIPLE TIMES AS NEEDED.)	
Race Consider identity, beliefs, and position within society's racial structure.	**Class** Consider identity, beliefs, and position within society's racial structure.
Gender Consider identity, beliefs, and how gender affected their opportunities.	**Religion** Consider identity, beliefs, and how religion affected their opportunities.

<table>
<tr><th colspan="2">INSERT ANCESTOR NAME HERE:</th></tr>
<tr><th colspan="2">CATEGORIZE YOUR FINDINGS ABOUT EACH ANCESTOR. (COPY AND USE THIS TABLE MULTIPLE TIMES AS NEEDED.)</th></tr>
<tr><td>Race
Consider identity, beliefs, and position within society’s racial structure.</td><td>Class
Consider identity, beliefs, and position within society’s racial structure.</td></tr>
<tr><td></td><td></td></tr>
<tr><td></td><td></td></tr>
<tr><td></td><td></td></tr>
<tr><td></td><td></td></tr>
<tr><td></td><td></td></tr>
<tr><td></td><td></td></tr>
<tr><td>Gender
Consider identity, beliefs, and how gender affected their opportunities.</td><td>Religion
Consider identity, beliefs, and how religion affected their opportunities.</td></tr>
<tr><td></td><td></td></tr>
<tr><td></td><td></td></tr>
<tr><td></td><td></td></tr>
<tr><td></td><td></td></tr>
<tr><td></td><td></td></tr>
<tr><td></td><td></td></tr>
</table>

INSERT ANCESTOR NAME HERE:	
CATEGORIZE YOUR FINDINGS ABOUT EACH ANCESTOR. (COPY AND USE THIS TABLE MULTIPLE TIMES AS NEEDED.)	
Race Consider identity, beliefs, and position within society's racial structure.	**Class** Consider identity, beliefs, and position within society's racial structure.
Gender Consider identity, beliefs, and how gender affected their opportunities.	**Religion** Consider identity, beliefs, and how religion affected their opportunities.

<table>
<tr><th colspan="2">INSERT ANCESTOR NAME HERE:</th></tr>
<tr><th colspan="2">CATEGORIZE YOUR FINDINGS ABOUT EACH ANCESTOR. (COPY AND USE THIS TABLE MULTIPLE TIMES AS NEEDED.)</th></tr>
<tr><th>Race
Consider identity, beliefs, and position within society’s racial structure.</th><th>Class
Consider identity, beliefs, and position within society’s racial structure.</th></tr>
<tr><td></td><td></td></tr>
<tr><td></td><td></td></tr>
<tr><td></td><td></td></tr>
<tr><td></td><td></td></tr>
<tr><td></td><td></td></tr>
<tr><td></td><td></td></tr>
<tr><th>Gender
Consider identity, beliefs, and how gender affected their opportunities.</th><th>Religion
Consider identity, beliefs, and how religion affected their opportunities.</th></tr>
<tr><td></td><td></td></tr>
<tr><td></td><td></td></tr>
<tr><td></td><td></td></tr>
<tr><td></td><td></td></tr>
<tr><td></td><td></td></tr>
<tr><td></td><td></td></tr>
</table>

INSERT ANCESTOR NAME HERE:	
CATEGORIZE YOUR FINDINGS ABOUT EACH ANCESTOR. (COPY AND USE THIS TABLE MULTIPLE TIMES AS NEEDED.)	
Race Consider identity, beliefs, and position within society's racial structure.	**Class** Consider identity, beliefs, and position within society's racial structure.
Gender Consider identity, beliefs, and how gender affected their opportunities.	**Religion** Consider identity, beliefs, and how religion affected their opportunities.

INSERT ANCESTOR NAME HERE:	
CATEGORIZE YOUR FINDINGS ABOUT EACH ANCESTOR. (COPY AND USE THIS TABLE MULTIPLE TIMES AS NEEDED.)	
Race Consider identity, beliefs, and position within society's racial structure.	**Class** Consider identity, beliefs, and position within society's class structure.
Gender Consider identity, beliefs, and how gender affected their opportunities.	**Religion** Consider identity, beliefs, and how religion affected their lives.

BIBLIOGRAPHY

A.A. World Services. (1967). *As Bill sees it*. Alcoholics Anonymous World Services.

A.A. World Services. (1976). *Alcoholics Anonymous: The story of how many thousands of men and women have recovered from alcoholism*. Author.

A.A. World Services. (1989). *Twelve steps and twelve traditions*. Author.

Alcoholics Anonymous. (2011 reprint). *Alcoholics Anonymous*. Dover. (Original work published 1939)

Abend, G. (2008). The meaning of "theory." *Sociological Theory, 26*(2), 173–199. https://doi.org/10.1111/j.1467-9558.2008.00324.x

Alexander, M. (2010). *The new Jim Crow*. New Press.

Allen, T. (2012a). *The invention of the White race: Racial oppression and social control* (Vol. 1). Verso.

Allen, T. (2012b). *The invention of the White race: Racial oppression and social control* (Vol. 2). Verso.

American Psychiatric Association. (2010). *Home page*. psychiatry.org.

Ankel, S. (2022, January 25). VA governor, who has banned CRT, launches tip line to report teachers. *Business Insider*. https://www.businessinsider.com/glenn-youngkin-launches-tipline-report-teachers-2022-1

Anderson, C. (2017). *White rage: The unspoken truth of our racial divide*. Bloomsbury.

Asch, C. M. (2008). *The senator and the sharecropper: The freedom struggles of James O. Eastland and Fannie Lou Hamer*. The New Press.

Avelino, F. (2021). Theories of power and social change. Power contestations and their implications for research on social change and innovation. *Journal of Political Power, 14*(3), 425–448. https://doi.org/10.1080/2158379x.2021.1875307

Baldwin, J., & Schapiro, S. (2019). *The fire next time* (N. Weiner, Ed.). Taschen. (Original work published 1962)

Baldwin, J. (2021). *The fire next time*. Modern Library. (Original work published 1962)

Baltzly, D. (2019). Stoicism. *Stanford encyclopedia of philosophy*. https://plato.stanford.edu/archives/spr2019/entries/stoicism/

Baptist, E. E. (2014). *The half has never been told: Slavery and the making of American capitalism*. Basic Books.

Battalora, J. (2021). *Birth of a White nation: The invention of White people and its relevance today*. Routledge.

BBC News. (2013, July 29). *Pope Francis: Who am I to judge gay people?* https://www.bbc.com/news/world-europe-23489702

Beckert, S. (2015). *Empire of cotton*. Penguin.

Beveridge, L. (2020, August 26). Civil rights activist Fannie Lou Hamer and opera singer Leontyne Price among inspiring women on Mississippi list. *USA Today*. https://www.usatoday.com/in-depth/life/women-of-the-century/2020/08/13/mississippi-woman-history-poet-author-activists-19th-amendment/5003960002/

Billington, J. (2019). *Exploring the Early Americas.* Library of Congress. https://www.loc.gov/exhibits/exploring-the-early-americas/columbus-and-the-taino.html

Boff, L. (1988). *When theology listens to the poor.* Harper & Row.

Bonikowski, B., & DiMaggio, P. (2016). Varieties of American popular nationalism. *American Sociological Review, 81*(5), 949–980. https://doi.org/10.1177/0003122416663683

Bourdieu, P. (1977). *Outline of a theory of practice.* Cambridge University Press. (Original work published 1972)

Bourdieu, P. (1984). *Distinction: A social critique of the judgement of taste.* Harvard University Press. (Original work published 1979)

Brandeis, L. D. (1915). *True Americanism.* Louis D. Brandeis School of Law Library. https://louisville.edu/law/library/special-collections/the-louis-d.-brandeis-collection/business-a-profession-chapter-22

Brennan Center for Justice. (n.d.). *Dark money.* https://www.brennancenter.org/issues/reform-money-politics/influence-big-money/dark-money

Brewster, F. (2019). *Archetypal grief: Slavery's legacy of intergenerational child loss.* Routledge.

Britannica Encyclopedia. (n.d.). *Sanatana dharma.* https://www.britannica.com/topic/sanatana-dharma

Brooks, E., Parker, C., Lin, N., Spievack, N., & Oxholm, P. (2022). *The structural racism remedies repository.* Othering & Belonging Institute. https://belonging.berkeley.edu/structural-racism-remedies-repository

Brown, D. A. (2021). *The Whiteness of wealth: How the tax system impoverishes Black Americans and how we can fix it.* Crown.

California Department of Education. (2021, February). *Current expense of education.* https://www.cde.ca.gov/ds/fd/ec/currentexpense.asp

Case, A., & Deaton, A. (2020). *Deaths of despair and the future of capitalism.* Princeton University Press.

Cashin, S. (2021). *White space, black hood: Opportunity hoarding and segregation in the age of inequality.* Beacon Press.

Center for Humane Technology. (n.d.). *Home page.* www.humanetech.com

Chetty, R., Friedman, J., Hendren, N., Jones, M. R., & Porter, S. R. (2018, October 1). *The opportunity atlas: Mapping the childhood roots of social mobility.* Opportunity Insights. https://opportunityinsights.org/paper/the-opportunity-atlas/

Chotiner, I. (2020, August 3). Why Stuart Stevens wants to defeat Donald Trump. *The New Yorker.* https://www.newyorker.com/news/q-and-a/why-stuart-stevens-wants-to-defeat-donald-trump

Clark, H., & Knowles, C. (2013). *Resolution in memory of Helga Burnham Watson.* Scott County Democratic Executive Committee.

Coates, T. (2017). *We were eight years in power: An American tragedy.* One World.

Cobb, J., & Zocalo Public Square. (2018, April 4). Even though he is revered today, MLK was widely disliked by the American public when he was killed. *Smithsonian Magazine.* https://www.smithsonianmag.com/history/why-martin-luther-king-had-75-percent-disapproval-rating-year-he-died-180968664/

Cokley, K. O. (2022). *Making Black lives matter: Confronting anti-Black racism.* Cognella Academic Publishing.

Communication Theory. (2014, July 10). *The Johari window model.* https://www.communicationtheory.org/the-johari-window-model/

Covey, S. R. (1989). *The seven habits of highly effective people: Restoring the character ethic*. Simon & Schuster.

Cronquist, K. (2020). *Characteristics of SNAP households: FY 2019*. U.S. Food and Nutrition Service. https://www.fns.usda.gov/snap/characteristics-snap-households-fy-2019

Dankasa, J. (2015). Developing a theory in academic research: A review of experts' advice. *Journal of Information Science Theory and Practice, 3*(3), 64–74. https://doi.org/10.1633/jistap.2015.3.3.4

Darity, W. A., & Mullen, K. A. (2020). *From here to equality: Reparations for Black Americans in the twenty-first century*. University of North Carolina Press.

David, E. J. R. (2013). *Brown skin, White minds: Filipino -/ American postcolonial psychology*. Information Age.

Davis, A. (2016). *Freedom is a constant struggle: Ferguson, Palestine, and the foundations of a movement*. Haymarket Books.

Davis, F. (2019). *The little book of race and restorative justice: Black lives, healing, and US social transformation*. Good Books.

Dearman, S. (2007, November 15). Ronald Reagan speech, Neshoba County Fair, 1980. *The Neshoba County Democrat*. https://neshobademocrat.com/stories/ronald-reagans-1980-neshoba-county-fair-speech,49123

DeGruy, J. (2005). *Post traumatic slave syndrome: America's legacy of enduring injury and healing*. Joy DeGruy Publications Inc.

Delpit, L. (2006). *Other people's children: Cultural conflict in the classroom*. New Press.

Deranty, J. P. (2016). Exploited: Exploitation as a subjective category. *The Southern Journal of Philosophy, 54*(S1), 31–43. https://doi.org/10.1111/sjp.12185

Diangelo, R. (2021). *Nice Racism: How Progressive White People Perpetuate Racial Harm*. Beacon.

Diangelo, R. J. (2018). *White fragility: Why it's so hard for White people to talk about racism*. Beacon Press.

DiMaggio, P. J. (1995). Comments on "What Theory Is Not." *Administrative Science Quarterly, 40*(3), 391–397. https://doi.org/10.2307/2393790

Dollard, J. (2010). *Caste and class in a southern town*. Yale University Press. (Original work published 1937)

Domhoff, W. G. (2017). *Studying the power elite: Fifty years of who rules America?* Taylor & Francis.

Doyle, W. (2001). *An American insurrection: The battle of Oxford, Mississippi, 1962*. Doubleday.

Editors of Encyclopedia Britannica. (n.d.). *Philosopher's stone*. https://www.britannica.com/topic/philosophers-stone

Fahle, E. M., Reardon, S. F., Kalogrides, D., Weathers, E. S., & Jang, H. (2020). Racial segregation and school poverty in the United States, 1999–2016. *Race and Social Problems, 12*(1), 42–56. https://doi.org/10.1007/s12552-019-09277-w

Fanon, F. (2004). *The wretched of the earth*. Grove Press. (Original work published 1961)

Fanon, F. (2008). *Black skin, White masks*. Grove Press. (Original work published 1952)

FBI History. (1964). *Mississippi burning*. https://www.fbi.gov/history/famous-cases/mississippi-burning

Feuerstein, G. (1989). *The yoga-sutra of Patanjali: A new translation and commentary*. Inner Traditions.

FindLaw. (n.d.). *What does "caveat emptor" mean?* https://www.findlaw.com/consumer/consumer-transactions/what-does-caveat-emptor-mean-.html

Fishkin, J., & Forbath, W. E. (2022). *The anti-oligarchy constitution: Reconstructing the economic foundations of American democracy.* Harvard University Press.

Floyd, I., Pavetti, L., Meyer, L., Safawi, A., Schott, L., Bellew, E., & Magnus, A. (2021, August 4). *TANF policies reflect racist legacy of cash assistance: Reimagined program should center Black mothers.* Center on Budget and Policy Priorities. https://www.cbpp.org/research/family-income-support/tanf-policies-reflect-racist-legacy-of-cash-assistance

Foner, E. (2019). *The second founding: How the Civil War and Reconstruction remade the Constitution.* Norton.

Fortin, J. (2021, November 8). Critical race theory: A brief history. *The New York Times.* https://www.nytimes.com/article/what-is-critical-race-theory.html

Freire, P. (1970). *Pedagogy of the oppressed* (M. Bergman Ramos, Trans.). Herder and Herder.

Gates, Jr., H. L. (2019). *Stony the road: Reconstruction, White supremacy, and the rise of Jim Crow.* Penguin Books.

Gates, Jr., H. L. (Ed.). (2021, December 20). *Maya Rudolph Reacts to Family History in Finding Your Roots | Ancestry.* www.youtube.com; Ancestry.com | Finding Your Roots. PBS. Host, Henry Louis Gates, Jr., Season 3 Episode 3, Clip. https://www.youtube.com/watch?v=WpkYo8YLeH8

George, J. (2021, January 12). *A lesson on critical race theory.* American Bar Association. https://www.americanbar.org/groups/crsj/publications/human_rights_magazine_home/civil-rights-reimagining-policing/a-lesson-on-critical-race-theory/

Ghaemi, N. (2017, July 24). The ghost of Barry Goldwater and the censorship of American psychiatrists. *Washington Monthly.* https://washingtonmonthly.com/2017/07/24/the-ghost-of-barry-goldwater-and-the-censorship-of-american-psychiatrists/

Giddings, P. (1984). *When and where I enter: The impact of Black women on race and sex in America.* William Morrow.

Glaude, Jr., E. S. (2017). *Democracy in Black: How race still enslaves the American soul.* Broadway Books.

Glaude, Jr., E. S. (2020). *Begin again.* Crown.

Goldberg, P. (2010). *American Veda: From Emerson and the Beatles to yoga and meditation: How Indian spirituality changed the West.* Harmony Books.

Goyette, K. A., & Lareau, A. (2014). *Choosing homes, choosing schools: Residential segregation and the search for a good school.* Russell Sage Foundation.

Graham, J. (2021). *Plantation theory: The Black professional's struggle between freedom & security.* Mynd Matters Publishing.

Gramsci, A., Buttigieg, J. A., & Callari, A. (2011). *Prison notebooks* (Vols. 1–3). Columbia University Press.

Graves, E. M., & Savage, S. A. (2015). *Promoting pathways to financial stability: A resource handbook on building financial capabilities of community college students.* The Federal Reserve Bank of Boston. https://www.bostonfed.org/publications/one-time-pubs/financial-capabilities-handbook.aspx

Greene, A., & Greene, A. (2015, January 20). Flashback: Neil Young covers "Sweet Home Alabama" in 1977. *Rolling Stone.* https://www.rollingstone.com/music/music-news/flashback-neil-young-covers-sweet-home-alabama-in-1977-186638/

Guénolé, F., Marcaggi, G., & Baleyte, J.-M. (2013). Do dreams really guard sleep? Evidence for and against Freud's theory of the basic function of dreaming. *Frontiers in Psychology, 4*. https://doi.org/10.3389/fpsyg.2013.00017

Gutiérrez, G. (1988). *A theology of liberation: History, politics, and salvation*. Orbis Books. (Original work published 1971)

Hannah-Jones, N., & New York Times Company. (2021). *The 1619 Project: A new origin story*. One World.

Harris, F., III, & Wood, J. L. (2021, February 12). Racelighting: A prevalent version of gaslighting facing People of Color. *Diverse: Issues in Higher Education*. https://www.diverseeducation.com/opinion/article/15108651/racelighting-a-prevalent-version-of-gaslighting-facing-people-of-color

Height, D. (2003). *Open wide the freedom gates: A memoir*. Public Affairs.

Helms, J. E. (2020). *A race is a nice thing to have: A guide to being a White person or understanding the White persons in your life*. Cognella.

Herbers, J. (1964, August 9). Neshoba County Fair unclouded by murder of rights workers. *The New York Times*. https://www.nytimes.com/1964/08/09/archives/neshoba-county-fair-unclouded-by-murder-of-rights-workers.html

hooks, b. (1989a). *Feminist theory: From margin to center*. South End Press.

hooks, b. (1989b). *Talking back: Thinking feminist, thinking Black*. South End Press.

hooks, b. (1996). *Teaching to transgress: Education as the practice of freedom*. Routledge.

hooks, b. (2001). *Salvation: Black people and love*. William Morrow.

hooks, b. (1996). *Killing rage: Ending racism*. Henry Holt and Company.

Hope, D., & Limberg, J. (2020). *The economic consequences of major tax cuts for the rich*. https://eprints.lse.ac.uk/107919/1/Hope_economic_consequences_of_major_tax_cuts_published.pdf

Isenberg, N. (2016). *White trash: The 400-year untold history of class in America*. Viking.

Jaccard, J., & Jacoby, J. (2020). *Theory construction and model-building skills: A practical guide for social scientists*. Guilford Press.

Janney, C. (n.d.). The lost cause. *Encyclopedia Virginia*. https://encyclopediavirginia.org/entries/lost-cause-the

Jones, R. P. (2020). *White too long: The legacy of White supremacy in American Christianity*. Simon & Schuster.

Kelly, J. T. (2012). *Framing democracy: A behavioral approach to democratic theory*. Princeton University Press.

Kendi, I. X. (2019). *How to be an antiracist*. One World.

King, M. L., Jr. (1967). *Beyond Vietnam: A time to break silence*. Common Dreams. https://www.commondreams.org/views/2018/01/15/beyond-vietnam-time-break-silence

King, M. L., Jr. (2010). *Why we can't wait*. Beacon Press. (Original work published 1963)

Klein, E. (2020). *Why we're polarized*. Avid Reader Press.

Kornfield, J. (2008). *Guided meditation: Six essential practices to cultivate love, awareness, and wisdom* [Album]. Sounds True.

Kozol, J. (1991). *Savage inequalities: Children in America's schools*. Crown Pub.

Krathwohl, D. R. (2002). A revision of Bloom's taxonomy: An overview. *Theory into Practice, 41*(4), 212–218. https://doi.org/10.1207/s15430421tip4104_2

Kraus, M. W., Rucker, J. M., & Richeson, J. A. (2017). Americans misperceive racial economic equality. *Proceedings of the National Academy of Sciences, 114*(39), 10324–10331. https://doi.org/10.1073/pnas.1707719114

Kuhn, M., Schularick, M., & Steins, U. I. (2020). Income and wealth inequality in America, 1949–2016. *Journal of Political Economy, 128*(9), 3469–3519. https://doi.org/10.1086/708815

Ladson-Billings, G. (2006). From the achievement gap to the education debt: Understanding achievement in U.S. schools. *Educational Researcher, 35*(7), 3–12. https://doi.org/10.3102/0013189x035007003

Lakoff, G. (1996). *Moral politics: What conservatives know that liberals don't.* University of Chicago Press.

Lareau, A. (2011). *Unequal childhoods: Class, race, and family life* (2nd ed.). University of California Press.

Lee, B. X. (2019). *The dangerous case of Donald Trump: 37 psychiatrists and mental health experts assess a president: Updated and expanded with new essays.* Thomas Dunne Books, an Imprint of St. Martin's Press.

Lee, J., Sleeter, C., & Kumashiro, K. (2015). Interrogating identity and social contexts through "critical family history." *Multicultural Perspectives, 17*(1), 28–32. https://doi.org/10.1080/15210960.2015.994426

Leonardo, Z. (2005). *Critical pedagogy and race.* Blackwell.

Leonardo, Z. (2009). *Race, Whiteness, and education.* Routledge.

Leonardo, Z. (2013). *Race frameworks: A multidimensional theory of racism and education.* Teachers College Press.

Levitsky, S., & Ziblatt, D. (2018). *How democracies die.* Crown.

Manji, I. (2019). *Don't label me: An incredible conversation for divided times.* St. Martin's Press.

Mann, M. (2012–2013). *The sources of social power* (Vol. 1–4). Cambridge University Press. (Original work published 1986)

Marsh, C. (1997). *God's long summer: Stories of faith and civil rights.* Princeton University Press.

The Martin Luther King, Jr. Center for Non-Violent Change. (2022). *The beloved community: The fierce urgency of now* [Video]. https://www.youtube.com/watch?v=aujrJRFyI34

Martin, M. (1987). *The Jesuits: The society of Jesus and the betrayal of the Roman Catholic Church.* Linden Press.

McDavid, I. R., Jr., & McDavid, V. G. (1969). The late unpleasantness: Folk names for the Civil War. *The Southern Speech Journal, 34*(3), 194–204. https://doi.org/10.1080/10417946909372004

McGhee, H. C. (2021). *The sum of us: What racism costs everyone and how we can prosper together.* One World.

Menand, L. (2018, January 18). Lessons from the election of 1968. *The New Yorker.* https://www.newyorker.com/magazine/2018/01/08/lessons-from-the-election-of-1968

Metzl, J. M. (2020). *Dying of Whiteness: how the politics of racial resentment is killing America's heartland.* Basic Books.

Miller, J. H. (1996). Kudzu eradication and management. In D. Hoots & J. Baldwin (Eds.), *Kudzu: The vine to love or hate* (pp. 137–149). Suntop Press.

Mills, C. W. (1956). *The power elite.* Oxford University Press.

Mills, C. W. (2000). *The sociological imagination.* Grove Press.

Mills, K. (1993). *This little light of mine: The life of Fannie Lou Hamer.* Dutton.

Mounk, Y. (2018). *The people vs. democracy: Why our freedom is in danger and how to save it.* Harvard University Press.

Newkirk, P. (2019). *Diversity, Inc.: The failed promise of a billion-dollar business.* Bold Type Books.

Nichols, J. (2010, November 11). The long goodbye. *The Economist.* https://www.economist.com/united-states/2010/11/11/the-long-goodbye

O., P. (1995). *There's more to quitting drinking than quitting drinking.* Sabrina Publishing.

O'Brian, E. G. (2018). *The jewel of abundance: Finding prosperity through the ancient wisdom of yoga.* New World Library.

Ownby, T. (2017). *Mississippi Action for Progress (MAP).* Center for Study of Southern Culture, Mississippi Encyclopedia. http://mississippiencyclopedia.org/entries/mississippi-action-for-progress/

Painter, N. I. (2011). *The history of White people.* Norton.

Park, S. C. (2018). The Goldwater rule from the perspective of phenomenological psychopathology. *Psychiatry Investigation, 15*(2), 102–103. https://doi.org/10.30773/pi.2018.01.25

Parmar, A., & Kaloiya, G. (2018). Comorbidity of personality disorder among substance use disorder patients: A narrative review. *Indian Journal of Psychological Medicine, 40*(6), 517–527. https://doi.org/10.4103/IJPSYM.IJPSYM_164_18

Parry, M. (2019, November 8). The trouble with Ole Miss. *The Chronicle of Higher Education.* https://www.chronicle.com/article/the-trouble-with-ole-miss/

Phillips, A. (2022, June 27). The sex-trafficking investigation that's zeroing in on Matt Gaetz, explained. *The Washington Post.* https://www.washingtonpost.com/politics/2022/01/27/sex-trafficking-allegations-matt-gaetz/

powell, j. a. (2015). *Racing to justice: Transforming our conceptions of self and other to build an inclusive society.* Indiana University Press.

powell, j. a. (2017, August 29). Othering and belonging: An embodied spiritual practice. *Deep Times: A Journal of Work That Reconnects.* https://journal.workthatreconnects.org/2017/08/29/othering-and-belonging-expanding-the-circle-of-human-concern/

powell, j. a., Menendian, S., & Ake, W. (2019). *Targeted universalism: Policy & practice.* https://belonging.berkeley.edu/sites/default/files/targeted_universalism_primer.pdf

Reich, R. B. (2019). *The common good.* Knopf.

Reich, R. B. (2021). *The system: Who rigged it, how we fix it.* Vintage.

Rev. (2021, June 23). *General Milley, Secretary Austin answer critical race theory questions from Matt Gaetz testimony: Transcript.* https://www.rev.com/blog/transcripts/general-milley-secretary-austin-answer-critical-race-theory-questions-from-matt-gaetz-testimony-transcript

Richardson, H. C. (2020). *How the South won the Civil War: Oligarchy, democracy, and the continuing fight for the soul of America.* Oxford University Press.

Roediger, D. R. (2018). *Working toward Whiteness: How America's immigrants became White: The strange journey from Ellis Island to the suburbs.* Basic Books.

Rohter, L. (1998, April 3). 4 Salvadorans say they killed U.S. nuns on orders of military. *The New York Times.* https://www.nytimes.com/1998/04/03/world/4-salvadorans-say-they-killed-us-nuns-on-orders-of-military.html

Rubin, V., & McAfee, M. (2021, September 9). Decentering Whiteness: Building for the movement tasks ahead. *Nonprofit Quarterly*. https://nonprofitquarterly.org/decentering-whiteness-building-for-the-movement-tasks-ahead/

Sadoff, J. H., Sadoff, R. L., & Needleman, L. (2011). *Pieces from the past: Voices of heroic women in civil rights*. Tasora Books.

Salvador, J. (2022, February 15). Dr. Dre asked about Eminem taking a knee during the Super Bowl halftime show. *Sports Illustrated*. https://www.si.com/extra-mustard/2022/02/15/dr-dre-says-nfl-had-no-problem-with-eminem-taking-knee-super-bowl-halftime-show

Satz, R. (1986). The Mississippi Choctaw: From the Removal Treaty to the federal agency. In S. J. Wells & R. Tubby (Eds.), *After removal, The Choctaw in Mississippi* (p. 7). University Press of Mississippi.

Scott County Times Online. (2018). Slaughter Legacy honored: Forest Alderman W. L. And Mrs. Olivia Kelley Slaughter honored (posthumously) by Jackson Tougaloo Alumni Club. *Scott County Times*. https://www.sctonline.net/front-page-slideshow-features/slaughter-legacy-honored#sthash.74ptwXBg.dpbs

Shontell, A. (2013, September 11). The last gift Steve Jobs gave to family and friends was a book about self realization. *Business Insider*. https://www.businessinsider.com/steve-jobs-gave-yoganandas-book-as-a-gift-at-his-memorial-2013-9

Sifton, E. (2003). *The serenity prayer: Faith and politics in times of peace and war*. Norton.

Sleeter, C. (n.d.). *Home page*. https://www.christinesleeter.org/critical-family-history

Sleeter, C. E. (2011). Becoming White: Reinterpreting a family story by putting race back into the picture. *Race Ethnicity and Education, 14*(4), 421–433. https://doi.org/10.1080/13613324.2010.547850

Sleeter, C. (2015). Multicultural curriculum and critical family history. *Multicultural Education Review, 7*(1–2), 1–11. https://doi.org/10.1080/2005615x.2015.1048607

Sleeter, C. E. (2018). *The inheritance: A novel*. Sleeter Publishing.

Sleeter, C. (2020). Critical family history: An introduction. *Genealogy, 4*(2), 64. https://doi.org/10.3390/genealogy4020064

Sleeter, C. E. (2021). *Family history in Black and White: A novel*. Brill Sense.

Sleeter, C. (2022). Federal education policy and social justice education. In T. K. Chapman & N. Hobbel (Eds.), *Social justice pedagogy across the curriculum: The practice of freedom* (2nd ed.). Routledge.

Smiley, T., & West, C. (2012). *The rich and the rest of us: A poverty manifesto*. Smileybooks.

Stanford University Law School. (2021). *ABA women trailblazer's project*. Robert Crown Law Library. https://abawtp.law.stanford.edu/exhibits/show/constance-i-slaughter-harvey/biography?_ga=2.110698829.914675179.1597941222-1936040103.1597615574

Steele, C. (2010). *Whistling Vivaldi: And other clues to how stereotypes affect us*. Norton.

Stevens, S. (2020). *It was all a lie: How the Republican Party became Donald Trump*. Knopf.

Stewart, S., III, Chui, M., Manyika, J., Julien, J. P., Hunt, V., Sternfels, B., Woetzel, J., & Zhang, H. (2021). *The economic state of Black America: What is and what could be*. https://www.mckinsey.com/~/media/mckinsey/featured%20insights/diversity%20and%20inclusion/the%20economic%20state%20of%20black%20america%20what%20is%20and%20what%20could%20be/the-economic-state-of-black-america-what-is-and-what-could-be-f.pdf

Stoute, B. J. (2017). Race and racism in psychoanalytic thought: The ghosts in our nursery. *The American Psychoanalyst, 51*(1). https://apsa.org/apsaa-publications/vol51no1-TOC/html/vol51no1_08.xhtml

Sullivan, C. (2002). *Rescuing Jesus from the Christians.* Trinity Press International.

Sullivan, C. (2004). *Why Beulah shot her pistol inside the Baptist Church.* NewSouth Books.

Sutton, J. (2008, November 11). *San Antonio Independent School District v. Rodriguez* and its aftermath. *Virginia Law Review.* https://www.virginialawreview.org/articles/san-antonio-independent-school-district-v-rodriguez-and-its-aftermath/

Takaki, R. T. (2008). *A different mirror: A history of multicultural America.* Back Bay Books.

Tan, A. S. (2021). *Who is racist? Why racism matters.* Cognella Press.

Tarasoff v. Regents of Univ. of Cal. 13 Cal. 3d 177, 118 Cal. Rptr. 129, 529 P.2d 553 (Cal. 1974)

Tatum, B. D., (2007). *Can we talk about race? And other conversations in an era of school resegregation.* Beacon Press.

Taylor, E., Gillborn, D., & Ladson-Billings, G. (2009). *Foundations of critical race theory in education.* Routledge.

The Nature Conservancy. (2019). *Journey with nature: Kudzu.* https://www.nature.org/en-us/about-us/where-we-work/united-states/indiana/stories-in-indiana/kudzu-invasive-species/

Toporek, R. L., & Ahluwalia, M. K. (2021). *Taking action: Creating social change through strength, solidarity, strategy, and sustainability.* Cognella Press.

Truth and Reconciliation Commission. (1998). *Final report.* https://www.justice.gov.za/trc/report/execsum.htm

University of Southern Mississippi Wesley Foundation. (n.d.). *Our history.* https://www.usmwesley.org/our-history

U.S. Department of Justice. (2021). *The U.S. Marshalls and the integration of the University of Mississippi.* U.S. Marshall Service. https://www.usmarshals.gov/history/miss/02.htm

U.S. Office of Energy Efficiency & Renewable Energy. (2016). *Fact #915: March 7, 2016 average historical annual gasoline pump price, 1929–2015.* https://www.energy.gov/eere/vehicles/fact-915-march-7-2016-average-historical-annual-gasoline-pump-price-1929-2015

Vespa, J., Medina, L., & Armstrong, D. (2020). *Demographic turning points for the United States: Population projections for 2020 to 2060 population estimates and projections current population reports.* U.S. Census. https://www.census.gov/content/dam/Census/library/publications/2020/demo/p25-1144.pdf

Villanueva, E. (2018). *Decolonizing wealth: Indigenous wisdom to heal divides and restore balance.* Berrett-Koehler.

Vitali, A. (2016, February 29). *Alabama's Jeff Sessions becomes first senator to endorse Trump.* NBC News. https://www.nbcnews.com/politics/2016-election/alabama-s-jeff-sessions-becomes-first-senator-endorse-trump-n527661

W, B., & Alcoholics Anonymous. (2019). *Alcoholics anonymous: The big book: The original 1939 edition.* Ixia.

Wakefield, J. C. (2015). DSM-5 substance use disorder: How conceptual missteps weakened the foundations of the addictive disorders field. *Acta Psychiatrica Scandinavica, 132*(5), 327–334. https://doi.org/10.1111/acps.12446

Wall Street Journal. (2016, November 15). Henry Louis Gates discusses ideological divides among Black Americans. https://www.wsj.com/video/henry-louis-gates-discusses-ideological-divides-among-black-americans/77306EFF-CDD0-425A-B47A-E07737846D57.html

Ward, L. (2020). *America's racial karma: An invitation to heal.* Parallax Press.

Watson, W., Esquivel-Swinson, A., & Montemayor, R. (2018). Collaborative impact and professional development: Effective student services for immigrant populations amid growing inequality. *Community College Journal of Research and Practice, 42*(11), 778–782. https://doi.org/10.1080/10668926.2018.1448727

Weber, M., & Tribe, K. (2019). *Economy and society a new translation.* Harvard University Press. (Original work published 1921)

Wells, S. J. (2014). *After removal: The Choctaw in Mississippi.* University Press of Mississippi.

West, C. (1994). *Race matters.* Beacon Press.

West, C. (2005). *Democracy matters: Winning the fight against imperialism.* Penguin Books.

Wilkerson, I. (2016). *The warmth of other suns: The epic story of America's great migration.* Random House.

Wilkerson, I. (2020). *Caste: The origins of our discontents.* Random House.

Williams, C. R. (2020, June 26). Opinion | You want a confederate monument? My body is a confederate monument. *The New York Times.* https://www.nytimes.com/2020/06/26/opinion/confederate-monuments-racism.html

Williams, P. (2020). The changing meaning of the American flag under Trump. *The New Yorker.* https://www.newyorker.com/news/us-journal/the-changing-meaning-of-the-american-flag-under-trump

Wilson, W. J. (2010). *More than just race: Being Black and poor in the inner city.* Norton.

Winter, W. F., & Mullins, A. P. (2006). *The measure of our days: Writings of William F. Winter.* William Winter Institute for Racial Reconciliation.

Wise, T. (2009). *Between Barack and a hard place: Racism and White denial in the age of Obama.* City Lights Books.

Wise, T. J. (2011). *White like me: Reflections on race from a privileged son: The remix.* Soft Skull Press.

Wise, T. (2020). *Dispatches from the race war.* City Lights Books.

Witness for Peace. (n.d.). *Home page.* https://www.witnessforpeace.org

Wolff, E. N. (2021). Household wealth trends in the United States, 1962 to 2019: Median wealth rebounds ... but not enough. *SSRN Electronic Journal.* https://doi.org/10.2139/ssrn.3772622

Wolff, T., Minkler, M., Wolfe, S., Berkowitz, B., Bowen, L., Butterfish, F. D., Christens, B. D., Francisco, V. T., Himmelman, A. T., & Lee, K. S. (2017, January 9). Collaborating for equity and justice: Moving beyond collective impact. *Nonprofit Quarterly.* https://nonprofitquarterly.org/2017/01/09/collaborating-equity-justice-moving-beyond-collective-impact/

Yogananda, P. (2008). *Autobiography of a yogi.* Self-Realization Fellowship. (Original work published 1946)

Yogapedia.com. (n.d.). *What is Aham Brahmasmi?* https://www.yogapedia.com/definition/8231/aham-brahmasmi

Zaragovia, V. (2014, October 1). *Cajuns are fiercely proud of their culture, but they're divided over the word "coonass."* The World. https://theworld.org/stories/2014-10-01/cajuns-are-fiercely-proud-their-culture-theyre-divided-over-word-coonass

Zehr, H. (2016). *The little book of restorative justice.* Langara College.

Zinn, H. (2015). *A people's history of the United States.* HarperPerennial.

Zwiers, M. (2018, May 25). Eastland, James O. *Mississippi Encyclopedia.* https://mississippiencyclopedia.org/entries/james-oliver-eastland/

About the Author

William Watson, EdD, first learned democracy watching his parents risk their lives (and his) in Mississippi during the 1960s Civil Rights Movement. Defying odds set by poverty and alcoholism, Dr. Watson earned degrees in philosophy and comparative religion, anthropology, and counseling psychology before earning a social justice–focused doctorate from San Francisco State University and completing a Presidential Fellowship for College Excellence with The Aspen Institute's partnership with Stanford University. After prototyping award-winning models of equity innovation in higher education for more than 20 years, he founded Waterbrook, a USA democracy project inspired by Martin Luther King Jr.'s *Beloved Community*. Waterbrook works for peace and prosperity through justice *then* liberty for all. Responding to James Baldwin's call in *The Fire Next Time* for new standards for White Americans, Watson wrote *Twelve Steps for White America: For a United States of America*, a provocative and hopeful treatment plan for democracy that envisions our best days ahead.

About the Contributor

Christine E. Sleeter, PhD, is professor emerita in the College of Education at California State University Monterey Bay. She is past president of the National Association for Multicultural Education, and past vice president (Division K) of the American Educational Research Association. Her research focuses on antiracist multicultural education, ethnic studies, teacher education, and critical family history. She has published more than 150 articles and 24 books. Awards for her work include the American Educational Research Association Social Justice in Education Award, the Chapman University Paulo Freire Education Project Social Justice Award, Kappa Delta Pi Laureate, and the National Association for Multicultural Education Exceptional Service Award. Dr. Sleeter was inducted into the National Academy of Education in 2020. Her latest book (coauthored with Francesca Lopez) is her fourth book for the James Banks' Teachers College Press series on multicultural education, *Critical Race Theory and Its Critics: Implications for Teaching and Research*.

www.ingramcontent.com/pod-product-compliance
Ingram Content Group UK Ltd.
Pitfield, Milton Keynes, MK11 3LW, UK
UKHW050144280726
14058UKWH00006B/819